FORT WORTH PUBLIC LIBRARY

3 1668 01120 2600

S0-BIR-019

FORT
WORTH
PUBLIC
LIBRARY

FORT W
PUBL

92 Hunter; Alvah Folsom
Hunter, Alvah Folsom, and the
A year on a monitor and the
destruction of Fort Sumter

A Year on a Monitor
and the
Destruction of Fort Sumter

A YEAR ON A MONITOR
AND THE

UNIVERSITY OF SOUTH CAROLINA PRESS

DESTRUCTION OF FORT SUMTER

by ALVAH FOLSOM HUNTER

Edited and with an Introduction by
Craig L. Symonds

Title Page Photograph:

The *Nahant* leads a stationary parade of monitors laid up in ordinary at League Island, New York, after the war (top). Called back into service for the Spanish-American War, the *Nahant* served as a harbor defense vessel (bottom). The extensive canvas tarp and other impedimenta on the afterdeck would be struck for battle. (U.S. Navy)

Copyright © University of South Carolina 1987
Published in Columbia, South Carolina, by the
University of South Carolina Press
Manufactured in the United States of America

Library of Congress Cataloging-in-Publication Data

Hunter, Alvah Folsom.
    A year on a monitor and the destruction of Fort
Sumter.

    (Classics in maritime history)
    Includes index.
    1. Hunter, Alvah Folsom. 2. Nahant (Ship) 3. Fort
Sumter (Charleston, S.C.) 4. United States—History—
Civil War, 1861–1865—Naval operations. 5. United
States—History—Civil War, 1861–1865—Personal
narratives. 6. Seamen—United States—Biography.
I. Symonds, Craig L. II. Title. III. Series.
E595.N33H86 1987   973.7′5 [B]   87-20971
ISBN 0-87249-531-0

CLASSICS IN MARITIME HISTORY
WILLIAM N. STILL, JR., EDITOR

What Finer Tradition: *Memoirs of Thomas O. Selfridge, Jr.,*
Rear Admiral, U.S.N.
by Thomas O. Selfridge, Jr.

Confederate Navy Chief: *Stephen R. Mallory*
by Joseph T. Durkin, S.J.

A Year on a Monitor and the Destruction of Fort Sumter
by Alvah Folsom Hunter
Edited and with an Introduction by Craig L. Symonds

CONTENTS

Illustrations

‖ Editor's Introduction

ALVAH FOLSOM HUNTER WAS BARELY SIXTEEN YEARS OLD AND
small for his age when in November of 1862 he appeared at the Navy
Recruiting Office in Boston and announced his intention to enlist in
the U.S. Navy as a "ship's boy." Alas, though the Navy was short of
able seamen to man the vessels of the rapidly growing blockade force,
it was overstocked with inexperienced "boys," and the "grizzled old
Commodore" in charge told him that there was no place for him. Not
one to be deterred so easily, Hunter returned again and again, badger-
ing the officials until he finally managed to convince Lieutenant David
B. Harmony, executive officer of the new monitor *Nahant*, that he
should be allowed to enlist.

As a result of his perseverance, young Alvah Hunter served one
full year aboard the *Nahant* (December 1862 to December 1863), and
during that time he kept a daily diary. Despite his youth—or perhaps
because of it—Hunter's journal jottings were characterized by a com-
pelling curiosity and keen powers of observation. Everything was new
to him: the strange habits of the men who shipped with him, the
routines of shipboard life, the curious iron vessel on which he served,
the warm southern winters, and of course the war itself. And he wrote
about them all. Despite a very limited formal education, Alvah Hunter
was bright and inquisitive, and inclined to investigate things that
aroused his curiosity. He was fascinated by the machinery of the
Nahant and made friends with the engineers so that they would let him

watch the mighty engine at work. He was interested enough in the Confederate shore fortifications to spend his one day of liberty ashore investigating a captured Confederate fort. He was even interested in the strategic decisions of when and how to neutralize Fort Sumter, matters well beyond the normal interests of a "ship's boy."

More than a half century later, as a septugenarian in the 1920s, Hunter sat down to turn the diary into a memoir, mostly for the benefit of his own grandchildren. He used the diary to jog his memory, but the vividness of his recollections is testimony to a remarkable mind. His brief diary entries sparked long stored-away visions of a particular sunset, or a storm-tossed coastline; the sudden appearance of a masked battery, or an afternoon ashore "blackberrying." The result is a first hand narrative of a year aboard an ironclad monitor during the Civil War that combines the freshness of an eyewitness account with the mature judgement of an older man.

Of course, Hunter's ebullient personality is evident throughout, and the narrative illuminates not only a great deal about the ironclad navy, but about Hunter as well. Like most young boys, he liked to swim and especially to fish. Indeed, fishing was a passion that he retained for all of his eighty-six years. He had fished the lakes and streams of New Hampshire before the war, and he fished from the deck of the *Nahant* during the blockade of Charleston. His love of fishing even aided the Union war effort on the day that a Confederate mine came floating down against the hull of the *Nahant*. It was young Alvah that spotted the "infernal machine" and called it to the attention of the deck officer. This was the vessel's first encounter with a rebel "torpedo," and all hands were equally ignorant as to how to proceed. Characteristically, it was Alvah who reached down to "feel" the line that led away from the floating keg into the murky depths. What terrible device might be at the end of it? While the ship's officers debated what to do, sixteen-year-old Alvah declared confidently that there was nothing at the end of the line for it felt slack "exactly like a fish-line with no sinker on the end. . . ." Fine, the deck officer told him, you pull it out. Rather sorry now that he had spoken up, Alvah nevertheless proceeded to draw up the line and was vindicated when the end of the line came up showing only an empty bight.

Another personal characteristic evident from the memoir is that Hunter was a bit of a Puritan. In particular he was an outspoken opponent of laziness, drunkenness, and idleness. He inherited his opposition to alcohol honestly. Hunter's paternal grandfather had been president of the Lincoln County Temperance Group in Maine and "all members of his family were total abstainers. . . ." There was never any liquor or tobacco in his own house and he never missed it. "In the varied course of my long life," he wrote, "I have seen much of the evil of intemperance, and I have frequently had occasion to voice my gratitude that I was brought up to total abstinence." In a revealing episode in this memoir, Hunter describes a confrontation that took place while he was exploring Morris Island during the siege of Charleston. Some Union soldiers who had managed to get their hands on a bottle of spirits, offered a "nip" to Hunter the sailor boy and were miffed when he refused. One of the soldiers, a big burley sort, announced his intention to force Hunter to be more sociable. Hunter was rescued from this fate by another soldier still sober enough to realize that if Hunter did not drink, there would be more left for the soldiers, and Hunter was therefore allowed to continue on his way. Clearly, in Hunter's mind, the incident represented a narrow escape from a danger that was, to him, as serious as enemy shells.

Hunter's wartime adventure began in the summer of 1861 when the entire nation was abuzz with talk of the Confederate firing on Fort Sumter. Even then, as a fourteen-year-old in tiny Gilford, New Hampshire, Alvah Hunter dreamed of a chance to go to war. He envied his older brother Charles, then sixteen, who was big enough, Alvah thought, to pass for eighteen. During that first summer of the war, while amateur armies clashed at Bull Run and General McClellan reorganized the shattered remnants of the defeated Union host, Alvah and Charles remained in New Hampshire helping their father try to make a go of a failing business. Times were hard. Alvah later recalled that "we found it hard, indeed, to get sufficient food to eat and clothes to wear." All the while he thought to himself: "Three years! If the war lasts for three years I can be in it, for I'll be eighteen years old in 1864!" "So tremendous was this thought to me," he later wrote, "for days and days I could think of little else."

When on July 11, 1862, Lincoln called upon the states for another 300,000 men to serve for three years, the residents of Belknap County determined to field their own regiment. As one after another of his friends and former schoolmates signed up, Alvah became obsessed with the idea of joining them. Finally it occurred to him that he might be taken as a drummer boy or a fife player. He recorded his effort to join the Union Army in an autobiographical account of his boyhood years, now in the hands of his grandchildren:

One day I went out to Laconia to do some errands and went into a recruiting office there. After some talk with Mr. Lane, the recruiting officer, I mentioned that I could play the fife after a fashion and he decided to enlist me and try to get me in as a musician. I was immensely elated, and gleefully told the folks at home that night that I had enlisted and was going to the war. During the two or three days that I was about home, I was quite a bit of a hero.

The state camp grounds were at Concord, but were so crowded with regiments that were assembling faster than uniforms and arms could be supplied, the Laconia company was ordered to go into camp on the fair grounds there, and we were encamped there, sleeping in the great exhibition hall, for something like two weeks. Then we boarded a train for Concord.

We were marched to a hall just off Main Street and each one was given a tin plate, cup, knife and fork and spoon. Then we marched across the valley and up the hill road to the plains, and there, in the camp ground, we were quartered in the barracks with the other companies of the 12th New Hampshire Infantry.

After something like two weeks, which were spent in company drill and one or two rather bungling attempts at lining-up as a regiment, we were ordered before the regimental surgeon for physical examination. I knew at once as I stood before the surgeon that my goose was cooked, for the surgeon was Dr. Charles Hunt, who had taught the school in Gilford Village and it was of no use to lie to him about my age—he knew me!

The . . . plan to find an opening as a musician was lost sight of, and all opportunities to go out as an officer's boy had been taken, so that afternoon another young chap from Laconia, Charles Chester by name, and I sorrowfully went over to Concord, were furnished with transportation to Laconia, and took the afternoon train for home.

But that was not the end of Alvah's efforts to join the "great adventure." Almost immediately he hit upon the idea of enlisting in the U.S. Navy. His age would still disqualify him from service as a seaman or even as an inexperienced "landsman," but the Navy also recruited "boys" to serve as stewards. In hopes of securing such a position, he left home for Boston at the beginning of November. There his persistence led him to the *Nahant* and his "year on a monitor."

The *Nahant* was a clone of the original *Monitor* that fought the C.S.S. *Virginia (Merrimack)* to a standstill in their famous engagement in Hampton Roads. That spectacular success led the Union government to order virtually dozens of these wonderful new vessels for the war. Hunter's *Nahant* was one of ten monitors of the *Passaic* class. It was 25 feet longer than the original *Monitor*, but virtually identical in design. In addition, the Union experimented with variations on this basic plan. In late 1862, about the time that Hunter joined the Navy, the government ordered nine monitors of a slightly improved type that were dubbed the *Canonicus* class, and the next year, the Union began construction of several very large ocean-going monitors that were never completed.

What all these vessels had in common was a remarkable invulnerability to shot and shell, and an equally remarkable unseaworthiness. Ugly and ungainly with their low freeboard and iron hull, these bizarre-looking fighting platforms were "ships" unlike any the world had seen before. Their usefulness was not in traditional blockade duty where they might be required to pursue swift and elusive blockade runners, but in combat against shore fortifications. The presumed invincibility of the monitors made them the key to Navy Department plans to force an entry into Charleston Harbor and batter Fort Sumter into submission. And that put Hunter very much at the center of things.

In 1863 Charleston was the single most important Atlantic seaport of the Confederacy. Other ports, such as Wilmington, North Carolina, may have been better entrepots for blockade runners, but Charleston was where the war had begun, and the rebel flag flying from Fort Sumter was a continuous and humiliating taunt. Moreover, Hunter's service on the *Nahant* coincided with some of the most historically significant confrontations on the South Atlantic coast.

The dominant mission of all Union vessels on the South Atlantic coast was blockade. Practically the first act of the national government after the onset of hostilities in the American Civil War was to declare the port cities in the rebellious states closed to trade. As an agricultural society, the South had to import much of the materials of modern war from overseas, particularly from Europe. In order to deny the Confederates this source, and to prevent the establishment of close diplomatic or economic links between the Confederacy and the European powers, the Lincoln administration announced on April 19, 1861, that the ports of seven southern states were closed to all outside traffic. A week later, the proclamation was extended to include North Carolina and Virginia, which had seceded in the interim. Some members of the administration worried that the use of the term "blockade" might imply government recognition of Confederate belligerency status, and so the government claimed simply that the ports were being "closed" to foreign trade for domestic reasons. But efforts to maintain this legalistic distinction were soon forgotten in the midst of a more serious problem: enforcing the blockade.

According to accepted international law, no nation was obliged to respect a "paper blockade." In other words, merely saying that the ports were closed was not enough. The Union government had to establish a naval force off the coast to prevent vessels from entering or leaving the port. In recognition of this necessity, Lincoln's proclamation promised that "a competent force will be posted so as to prevent entrance and exit of vessels from the ports. . . ." But the U.S. Navy in 1861 was far too small to fulfill this promise. The Confederacy boasted over 3,500 miles of coastline, and the Navy Register of 1861 listed only ninety warships in commission, many of them patently unsuitable for blockade duty. The administration therefore embarked on a crash program of ship construction and purchase. By December of 1862 when Alvah joined the *Nahant*, the U.S. Navy could boast a total of 264 warships, a three-fold increase in a single year. One year later when Hunter left the Navy, he left behind a Navy of 427 warships. This armada was divided into four blockading squadrons: The East and West Gulf Squadrons, and the North and South Atlantic Squadrons. Hunter's vessel served in the South Atlantic Squadron under the command, initially at least, of Flag Officer Samuel F. Du Pont.

Hunter's service aboard the *Nahant* involved him in many of the most important engagements of the South Atlantic Squadron. In particular, he was a participant in and a witness to the ill-judged and ill-fated attack on Fort Sumter on April 7, 1863. Although Du Pont's fleet had captured Port Royal, South Carolina, the previous November with little difficulty, the defenses there had consisted only of hastily erected earthworks. This time the thick masonry walls of Fort Sumter and the skill of the Confederate gunners proved too much for Du Pont's fleet—despite the ironclads. The *Nahant* was pounded by the heavy guns of Fort Sumter—struck 36 times in a matter of minutes. One shot smashed into the pilothouse and jarred loose a bolt which ricocheted about the inside of the pilothouse wounding two men (including the captain, John Downes) and killing the helmsman. Hunter's account of the day's combat reinforces the view of most historians that Du Pont's decision not to renew the action after his initial repulse was wise. Nevertheless, because Washington had counted so heavily on the Navy's success, a scapegoat was necessary for the failure and Du Pont was the only available candidate. He was soon replaced by Rear Admiral John A. Dahlgren.

Learning from Du Pont's experience, Dahlgren did not attempt to force his way into the harbor past Fort Sumter and its obstructions, but he did use his monitors—including the *Nahant*—against the Confederate defenses on Morris Island, including powerful Fort Wagner. Hunter's memoir includes an account of the Navy's nearly continuous bombardment of Wagner, and the Army's simultaneous attack across the sandy beaches of Morris Island. That attack, led by two black regiments, resulted in the repulse of the Union forces and the death of the commander of the Fifty Fourth Massachusetts Infantry (Colored), Colonel Robert Shaw. But continued bombardment wore down the defenders and eventually the Confederates were forced to evacuate. Adventurous youth that he was, Hunter used his liberty day ashore to explore the captured Confederate fort that had been the target of the *Nahant*'s guns.

Hunter's narrative is also useful for what it illuminates about the rapid technological changes that took place during the war. In addition to learning what he could about the mechanical mysteries of the monitors themselves, Hunter had to be on guard for repeated Confederate attempts to overcome Union numerical superiority with technological innovation. The ironclad *Virginia* had proven a great success against traditional wooden warships in Hampton Roads, and Confederate planners were eager to construct more ironclads of a similar design. In June 1863, the casemated ironclad *Atlanta*, converted at Savannah from the blockade runner *Fingal*, was finally ready for sea and moved ponderously into Wassaw Sound. As fate would have it, the two vessels blocking her path were the monitors *Weehawken* and *Nahant*. In a brief, violent confrontation the *Weehawken* secured the *Atlanta*'s surrender. Though many observers then and since have concluded that this battle demonstrated the superiority of turreted vessels to casemated ironclads, Hunter's conclusion is that the outcome of the battle was less a result of inferior technology than the product of inferior tactics. The officers of the *Atlanta*, he wrote, "committed a fatal blunder when they stopped her engine and awaited the approach of the *Weehawken*." In fact, the *Atlanta* had run aground and lay a hapless target for the guns of the *Weehawken*.

Another Confederate technological innovation was the dreaded "torpedo" or "infernal machine" several of which the Confederates placed in the harbor as obstructions or used more daringly as offensive weapons. Kegs filled with black powder and triggered by a mechanical device were affixed to the end of a long spar protruding from the bow of small semi-submerged vessels called "David" boats. The crews of such vessels sought to place their torpedo against the side of a Union vessel and then to detonate it. Volunteers for such service did not expect to survive, but the very existence of such vessels put fear in the hearts of the blockaders who were required to keep a careful watch night and day.

The most ubiquitious danger to Union sailors was posed by the iron warships in which they served. German U-boat sailors in World War I called their vessels "iron coffins," but the term might also have been applied to the ponderous monitors. The original *Monitor* went down in a storm off Cape Hatteras in December 1862, and Hunter was a horrified eyewitness to the sinking of the *Weehawken*, a sister ship of the *Nahant*, which went to the bottom in calm waters on a sunny day off Charleston when the water in her bilge overcame her small reserve bouyancy. Hunter recalled the words of the old sailor aboard the *Ohio* who had warned him: "You'll all go to the bottom in her, youngster, that's where you'll all go."

Hunter had been fully prepared to re-enlist for another year, but the plunge of the *Weehawken* led him to change his mind. It was not, however, the end of his military service. After he left the Navy, Hunter joined the U.S. Army Signal Corps where he served in the lower Mississippi River area until the end of the war. But though he had traveled through twenty states before he was eventually discharged in the exotic city of New Orleans, none of his Army adventures matched those of his year in the Navy.

After the war, Hunter enrolled at New Hampton Academy for his only formal education beyond grammar school. However, he was restless, and left after a year or so. Little is known of his means of livelihood for the next sixteen years. One of his endeavors was promoting a printing process, an activity which took him to Europe twice for extended periods. He married Alice Thurston in 1872 and with her raised a family of four sons. In 1883, he started a poultry business, and soon owned a large poultry farm. Eventually, he became the editor of two journals on farming and poultry raising. At the end of World War I, he retired and moved to West Roxbury, Massachusetts, not far from his boyhood home in New Hampshire, where he could return to his early love—fishing. In the 1920s he wrote two memoirs—"A New

Hampshire Boyhood," and "A Year on a Monitor," which he completed about 1924. In 1932 he entered the old Soliders Home in Washington, D.C., and he died in 1933 at the age of 86.

＊　＊　＊

Because it is an original document—even though it was written down some sixty years after the fact—I did not want to wield a heavy editorial pen in preparing Hunter's manuscript for publication. I have therefore interfered as little as possible in the original syntax of Hunter's manuscript. The text is very heavy in its reliance on the passive voice, but this was Hunter's choice and I have allowed it to stand. I did, however, make some minor corrections. First, because Hunter often strung together several sentences with semicolons, I replaced many of his semicolons with periods. In the same spirit I less frequently lumped together some very short single-sentence paragraphs into one longer paragraph when it seemed appropriate to do so. Second, in checking the accuracy of the quotations that Hunter cites from nineteenth-century sources, I discovered that he occasionally made small errors in transcription. These I have silently corrected. Finally, I chose to omit a very long quotation from John Johnson's *Defense of Charleston Harbor* which Hunter had included in Chapter 12. The passage seems to have been included in the first place because it confirmed Hunter's memory rather than because it added anything new. With these exceptions, and the addition of the footnotes, the manuscript is exactly as Hunter wrote it.

I would like to thank Gilbert Hunter, Alvah's grandson, for his help in the preparation of this manuscript for publication. In particular he made available to me Alvah's charming memoir of "A New Hampshire Boyhood," part of which is quoted above.

Craig L. Symonds
Annapolis, Maryland

A Year on a Monitor
and the
Destruction of Fort Sumter

1 ‖ Getting into the Navy

"**N**o!" said the grizzled old Commodore in charge of the naval recruiting office in North Square, Boston, before whose desk I was standing. "No, we can't ship any more boys. Why, the old *Ohio* is full of boys, there are more than two hundred boys on board of her now, and my orders are to 'ship no more boys till those have been drawn for service!' "[1]

This was the third time I had been given audience with the Commodore in the more than three weeks that I had been hanging around the North Square recruiting office, Boston, in November, 1862, and the decision seemed to be final. What more could I do? I had been baffled in my attempts to get into the army during the summer, having been rejected at the final examination, and after having been in camp with a company of a New Hampshire infantry regiment for about a month. It was then three months to my sixteenth birthday, and I was rejected because of being under age and of rather small size.

Returning home for a few weeks, I had helped in finishing up the fall work, then came down to Boston intending to ship in the navy as a boy, only to be told that no more boys could be enlisted. The orderly in charge of the anteroom of the recruiting office had told me it was of

---

1. The *Ohio* was a ship-of-the line authorized in 1817 and launched in 1820. It was placed in ordinary in 1840 and used as a receiving ship in Boston until it was recalled for service in the war with Mexico. Returned to Boston in 1850, it remained there as a receiving ship until 1875. With its guns removed, the two full gundecks provided ample space to house Navy recruits.

no use to try, that they already had more boys than there were places for. When I had gained audience with the chief clerk he had told me the same thing, and when I wouldn't be convinced and must needs see the Commodore, he had told me that no more boys could be shipped for a year at least.

It seemed unbelievable that an able-bodied youth who really *wanted* to get into the service should be shut out. President Lincoln's repeated calls for men showed that more and yet more help was needed. I had seen two or three score of my former schoolmates but two or three years older than myself put on the blue uniforms and march away to the front, and I, because of being only sixteen years old and rather small and slender for that age, was told again and again that I wasn't wanted. What could I do?

Talking the matter over with good Aunt Folsom,[2] and telling her of my great disappointment, she recalled that there were three or four other naval recruiting offices, one right there in Charlestown, another over in South Boston, etc. All these were visited in turn, only to learn that they were but ouposts of the chief recruiting office in North Square, and they all told that no more boys were wanted.

Day after day I had continued to hang about the rooms of the North Square recruiting office, and twice before I had succeeded in gaining admittance to the presence of the aged Commodore. On this third interview I made bold to tell him of my efforts to get into the army, and had attracted his sympathy to the extent that he kindly advised me to look for an opportunity to go to sea for a year or such a matter in the merchant service, and by that time, when I would be a year older and considerably stronger, I could ship in the navy as an "ordinary seaman" at considerably better wages, and there would then be no question of my getting into the navy. "Get into a good ship," he had said, "Keep your eyes open, learn to 'hand, reeve and steer', come back a year from now and you'll get into the navy all right."

That afternoon I went over to Chelsea for an over-Sunday visit at Aunt Hatch's.[3] She was the wife of a well-known ship captain, and had recently moved with her family into her fine, new house just at the foot of Powder Horn Hill. In my talks with Aunt Hatch I told of the old Commodore's advice that I go to sea in the merchant service for a year,

2. Celinda Folsom was married to Alvah's Uncle Dudley. In the fall of 1862 they lived on Irving Street in Boston.

3. Alvah's Aunt Sarah was married to William Hatch, a successful merchant caption. They lived in a "considerably greater style" than most of the Hunter relatives.

and asked her when Uncle William would be back from his voyage. It would probably be three or four months before Captain Hatch's ship would be back in New York, "And I think it would be much better for you to go to sea with a stranger captain than with a relative," she said. "You would then be standing upon your own feet entirely and would not be tempted to lean upon your uncle. You would be far more independent if standing alone, and would learn more." After thinking the matter over a little, Aunt Hatch said: "There's a new ship over in East Boston which will be going to sea quite soon. She's the *Stars and Stripes,* and you might get the chance to go out in her as a cabin boy. She was built down in Waldoboro and struck on the bar when being towed out of the river; her fore-foot was sprung, and she is up on the ways at Blank's ship yard having the damage repaired. It wouldn't be a bad idea for you to go over to East Boston to find out about her, and if you go there in the forenoon you'd probably find Captain Graves there."[4]

Acting upon this suggestion I visited Blank's ship yard a day or two later, and was so fortunate as to find there the captain of the *Stars and Stripes.* A half-hour's talk with him, in which I made use of Captain Hatch's name and told that he was my uncle, won for me the promise of the cabin boy's berth if I would wait the two weeks that it would require to get the ship ready for sea. "Come over and see me about the middle of next week and we'll fix it up," said Captain Graves, and my heart was much lightened by this promise of service of a kind, even if it wasn't the goal of my great desire.

Every day I visited the North Square recruiting office, in the hope that something favorable might turn up. I had not talked much with the attendants and hangers-on there, but some of them had come to know who I was, and they knew that I was very desirous to ship into the navy.

As I walked into the anteroom one morning a man came up to me and said: "You've been hangin' 'round here for some time tryin' to get into the navy, haven't yer?" I acknowledged that I had, and told [him] that I wanted to get into the navy very much indeed. "Wall," he said, "I think I can put yer into a way to get into the navy as a boy, and you're not stout enough to ship as anything else. Now, there's a new ship bein' built over at Loring's ship yard in South Boston, and she's

4. This vessel should not be confused with the U.S. Navy's Mystic-built screw steamer *Stars and Stripes* which was purchased into the service in the fall of 1861.

just about ready to be launched. She's one of the new monitors, the *Nahant*. Wall, if I help yer to get a place on her I'll get a dollar out of it, see?" I assured him that I could "see," but my glistening eyes must have told him much better than the spoken word.

"Wall," said my new friend, "My name's Higgins. Remember that, now." I nodded. "There's an officer detailed here for duty in lookin' after the buildin' of the *Nahant,* and he's goin' out in her as 'Executive Officer'. His name's Harmony. Now, you go over to Loring's ship yard in South Boston and ask to see Mr. Harmony. When he asks yer what yer want you tell him yer want to be shipped for the *Nahant,* to be a wardroom boy in her. He'll probably say that they don't need any more boys in the navy, but you just hang to him; you tell him you've tried and tried to get into the service, and tell him that you just *want* to go out in his ship. If you tell yer story right, now, he'll take yer."

Here, at last, seemed to be a door that might be opened, and I at once tramped off across Boston and over the bridge to South Boston. A policeman directed me down a long street to City Point, and I walked into the office of Loring's ship yard only to be told that Mr. Harmony wasn't expected to come to the works that day. Further inquiry revealed that Mr. Harmony was stopping at the Revere House, in the city, and that I might possibly find him there about lunch time, but they thought it was his intention to go out of town for the day.

At the office of the Revere House, I was told that Mr. Harmony was out, over at the navy yard they thought, and that they didn't know when he would be in. Yes, I might sit down there in the office and wait for him. About four o'clock in the afternoon, a military-looking gentleman walked to the desk and after a minute's conversation with the clerk he turned to me and asked: "Do you wish to speak to me?"

In as brief time as possible I told him the purpose of my call, told how I had tried to get into a navy and failed, and how I had been advised to apply to him to have me shipped especially for service on board the *Nahant.* Mr. Harmony listened courteously to my story, asked me several questions, and then said: "I'm afraid that you are not the kind of boy that we want for wardroom work, you seem to be too smart a boy for such service. We don't need smart boys to do the work in the wardroom." I told him that I wanted to go to the war, Oh! so much! And that I *had* hoped he would give me the coveted opportunity, and "wouldn't he *please* have me shipped for service on the

Nahant?" After some further talk, Mr. Harmony consented to take me, and said: "I'm going to be down at the recruiting office tomorrow morning, and if you'll meet me there about ten o'clock I'll have you shipped for the *Nahant.*"

An hour ahead of the appointed time I was at the recruiting office, and sat watching the door to see Mr. Harmony come in. Ten o'clock, ten-thirty, eleven o'clock, eleven-thirty, and no Mr. Harmony. To the Revere House I went again and was told that Mr. Harmony had been obliged to go out of the city, but would probably be back by four or five o'clock. Again I sat down and waited.

The hours seemed long, and it was already growing dark when Mr. Harmony walked in. Upon the clerk's telling him that I was waiting to see him he turned to me and told that he had been ordered to attend to some business of the Navy Department in another city which obliged him to go away by an early train, hence he could not meet me as promised. Then he took out his card case, drew out a card and wrote something on the back of it, handed the card to me and said: "If I'm unable to get down to the recruiting office tomorrow morning, just hand this card to the Commodore and he will ship you." Thanking him for his kindness I withdrew, and as soon as outside the door I looked at the car. On the back of it was written: "Ship this boy for the *Nahant.* D.B.H."

This looked as though my troubles were at an end, and that night I scarcely slept so great was my delight over the prospect. The next morning I was at the recruiting office before ten o'clock. I waited for over an hour, then asked the orderly to take me in to the Commodore. The old gentleman read the card, looked at me and half smiled as he drew a shipping blank towards him and began asking me questions.

He felt that it was his duty to grumble a bit, declaring that there were more boys aboard the *Ohio* now than there would be places for in a year's time, but the process of shipment was soon over and I was enrolled in the United States Navy as a First-Class Boy, shipped especially for service on board the U.S.I.C.S. *Nahant.* The initials stand for "United States Iron Clad Steamer, *Nahant.*" This was on the ninth day of December, 1862.

A brief physical examination was given me by a surgeon; probably a "boy" wasn't of sufficient importance to require a close examination. Then I was conducted to the outfitting room, where I was supplied with a uniform, two blue flannel shirts, socks, etc. in a clothes bag, a hammock with hair mattress and a pair of blankets, and in due time a dozen of us recruits were marched across the bridge to Charlestown, into the navy yard and ferried out to the receiving ship *Ohio.*

My clothes bag and hammock were marked with the number set against my name on the ship's muster roll, the hammock stowed in the hammock-netting above the rail, and I was conducted below to be given opportunity to change my shore clothes for my sailor's uniform. By the time this had been accomplished, the boatswain's whistle called to supper, and with the eating of that first meal aboard ship, I began to feel that at last I was really shipped into the navy.

For almost three weeks the old *Ohio* was my home, and I was so well content with having at last found a way into the navy I was quite satisfied to remain on board. The *Ohio* was an old Line-of-battle-Ship, with what seemed to me countless portholes for guns on three decks, and her vast bulk was a great attraction to my unaccustomed eyes. I passed hours roaming about her great decks, studying the fittings of a war ship, and watching the boys at their different games and diversions. There were some three or four hundred people on board, and probably two-thirds of them were boys of sixteen to eighteen years. A great many of these, however, had shipped as "landsmen," as I afterwards learned, chiefly because a landsman was paid two dollars more per month than a boy was paid. The wages of a "first-class boy" were eight dollars per month.

Marines were standing guard at the gangway, on the poop, by the cabin door, etc. One of the first things taught me was that a marine was the natural enemy of every sailor, and that all sailors were in duty bound to get ahead of the marines whenever possible. There were a score or more of decrepit old sailors aboard, whose duty it seemed to be to keep the youngsters in order, no light task with such a swarm of mischievous boys. The food was abundant and good, and there was little for us to do but turn out at six o'clock in the morning, sweep the decks, eat our three meals, and turn in after hammocks were piped down at eight bells (eight o'clock) in the evening.

Once a week we had a washing day, when we washed our clothes and hung them on clothes lines swung between the masts, and once a week the pumps were manned and the decks washed down, an occasion of much skylarking on the part of the boys and distress of the old sailors who directed the performance.

One bright, sunny afternoon I was sitting in a porthole on the starboard side of the gun deck looking out over the harbor, when my eyes were attracted to an odd-looking vessel steaming slowly along toward the navy yard, and I instantly recognized her to be the *Nahant*, my future home. One of the old sailors came up to look out of the porthole and I gleefully called his attention to the *Nahant* out there on the water, and told him I had shipped especially to go out in her. He burst out in a storm of profane abuse of "the bloody old tub," as he called her, and he declared "Them new-fangled iron ships ain't fit for hogs to go to sea in, let alone honest sailors! You'll all go to the bottom in her, youngster, there's where you'll all go!"

The next day, December 29th, the call was passed for the crew drawn for the *Nahant* to muster aft on the spar deck, and as soon as the roll had been called, we were ordered to get our bags and hammocks and stand ready to go to the new ship. Half an hour later we went over the side and were ferried ashore, then marched down the yard to the dock where the *Nahant* was moored, and filed on board. Bags and hammocks were stowed in the bag-and-hammock-rooms and all hands set to work clearing up the ship. Carpenters were still at work upon different unfinished parts, especially in the cabin and wardroom, and bushels of chips and shavings were gathered up and carried aft to the fire-room, where they could be used for kindlings.

There were four of us boys in the wardroom. Luckily for me one of these, a colored boy named George Patterson, had served for about a year on the gunboat *Huron*, and another, Barney Doyle, had been a dining-room waiter at the Revere House. They were both competent and willing to instruct me in my new duties.

There were ten officers' staterooms arranged around the ends and sides of a central "living-room." Three boys were given charge of the staterooms and waited upon the mess table during meals, the fourth boy, Dennis Doyle, was detailed to do the pantry work, wash dishes, etc., and assist the wardroom steward. The steward, who was our "boss", was a young man of German parentage named Kruger, and I found myself the only wardroom servant who was a Yankee.

It was near mid-afternoon when we came on board and had found out where we belonged, and before six o'clock we boys had the staterooms tidied up, berths made up for the night, and the table set for supper, which was served at six o'clock. After the officers had finished their meal we boys sat down at the table and ate our supper.

On the berth deck the crew had been equally busy under the superintendence of the boatswain's mate, a former English man-of-war's-man named Vincent, and at three bells (5:30 o'clock) the crew squatted on the deck, grouped around their several "mess cloths" for supper. At eight bells (eight o'clock), hammocks were piped out, each man slung his hammock from the hooks which bore his ship's number, and before two bells (nine o'clock) we had turned in for the night.

One of the watch-officers and one of the quartermasters was constantly on watch on the main deck, the watch being changed every four hours. The *Nahant* had been put in commission that day, with all of her officers present for duty. The officers were:

Official Rank.	Name.	Office on the Nahant.
Commander,	John Downes,	Captain.
Lieut. Commander,	David B. Harmony	Lieut. Commander & Executive Officer.
Acting Master,	William W. Carter,	Sailing Master & Watch officer
Acting Ensign,	Charles E. Clark,	Watch officer.
Acting Ensign,	Charles C. Ricker,	Watch officer.
Assistant Surgeon,	C. Ellery Stedman,	Surgeon.
Assistant Paymaster,	Edwin Putnam,	Purser.
1st Ass't Engineer,	F. J. Lovering,	Chief Engineer.
2d Ass't Engineer,	T. N. Bordley,	1st Ass't Engineer.
3d Ass't Engineer,	Abel Mitchener,	2d Ass't Engineer.
3d Ass't Engineer,	W. S. Neal,	3d Ass't Engineer.

2 ‖ GETTING ACQUAINTED WITH THE *NAHANT*

F OR THREE DAYS THE *NAHANT* LAY AT THE DOCK IN THE Charlestown navy-yard, the crew "finding itself" and busy taking aboard and stowing ordinance stores, provisions, etc. We boys were busy at what were to be our regular duties, and helping the steward unpack and stow upon the pantry shelves and in lockers scores of dozens of canned meats, fruits, vegetables and sauces, which were later to be served upon the wardroom table. Each forenoon and afternoon I could manage to get some little time for exploring the ship, and the more I studied the arrangement of rooms, lockers, the necessary "offices," etc., the more ingenious they seemed to be.

The *Nahant* was one of a fleet of some fifteen single-turreted monitors, which were ordered built directly after the great success of the *Monitor* in her battle with the *Merrimack* in Hampton Roads, Virginia, March 9, 1862. These new monitors were built at different points on the Atlantic coast and were given individual local names. Thus, the *Nahant* and *Nantucket* were built at Boston, the *Weehawken, Passaic, Catskill,* etc. at (or near) New York, the *Lehigh,* etc. at Philadelphia, the *Patapsco,* etc, at Baltimore.[1]

These monitors were a little larger than the *Monitor,* and differed from her in one very important point: the pilot house was set above the

---

1. The Union government built a total of ten monitors of the *Passaic* class which included the *Nahant.* Those not named by Hunter were the *Camanche, Montauk,* and *Sangamon.* In addition, the Union built nine single-turreted monitors of the *Canonicus* class.

11

top of the turret. They were also armed with heavier guns. They were planned to carry two XV—inch guns each as against two XI-inch guns in the *Monitor*, but unfortunately, the gun-works were unable to turn out those great guns as rapidly as the monitors were being built, which resulted in each monitor being armed with one XV-inch and one XI-inch gun. Two or three of the fleet were each given a 150-pounder Parrott rifled gun in place of the XI-inch smooth bore gun.

These new monitors were 200 feet long over all and 45 feet broad in the broadest part. They were 25 feet longer and 4-½ feet broader than the *Monitor*. These dimensions apply to the main deck, the "roof," so to speak, of the ship. The hull, or "body", of the ship was forty-one feet shorter and seven-feet-four inches narrower than the deck, and the extension of the deck beyond the hull was called "the overhang".

The hull was built of half-inch-thick iron plates strongly bolted to the frame, which was made of formed angle-iron stoutly braced. The ribs of the frame was eighteen inches apart on centres. The overhang was five feet deep, built of solid oak timbers, and was faced all along each side with four inches of iron armor, put on in inch-thick plates with edges overlapping and strongly bolted together. The bow and stern curved inward and the deck was sharply pointed at both ends. The forward overhang extended fifteen feet and the after overhang twenty-five feet beyond the hull, the greater extension aft being for the protection of the propeller and rudder.

The overhang was an important part of the "armor" of the vessel; it was a perfect protection to the hull. The hull curved inward and downward from where it left the overhang, and any shot to touch the hull would have to enter the water thirty or forty feet distant from the side of the ship, hence the force of the shot would be wholly spent before it reached the hull.

Clear forward in the bow, in the forward overhang, was a small circular apartment called the anchorwell, in which the four-fluked anchor hung free, the chain passing inboard over two iron wheels to the capstan, which was hung close to the deck above. The two capstan-arms extended down into the windlass-room so that they could be conveniently worked by the men, and they looked considerably like the pumping-arms of a hand-fire-engine. The anchor chain was coiled down in lockers beneath the floor of the windlass-room, and a ladder led from this room up through a small hatchway to the deck. When we were in habor and the hatches could be left off, this ladder was the captain's private companionway to the deck.

Next aft of the windlass-room was the captain's cabin, a snug dining-living room in the centre, a stateroom on one side and a pantry and a bath-room on the other. Doors from this cabin opened forward into the windlass-room and aft into the wardroom.

The wardroom was the quarters of the commissioned officers below the captain. There was a large dining-living room in the centre extending athwartship, the mess table being in the centre and ten staterooms and a wardroom pantry disposed around the sides. Each stateroom had a berth with capacious drawers for stowing clothing beneath, a lavatory, etc. A passageway led forward to the door of the captain's cabin and another passageway opened aft to the berthdeck.

The berthdeck was the living-room of the crew, and was a room about thirty by forty feet in size, with hooks in the beams overhead from which the men hung their hammocks at night. Against the forward partition which separated the berthdeck and wardroom were racks of rifles, revolvers, and cutlasses. The upper third of this partition was of lattice work, so that the air current, (which was forced forward to the windlass-room through two shafts beneath the deck by two blowers located in the turret-chamber), could flow aft, to pass out through the turret-chamber and up through the turret. This forced air current was the method of ventilating the forward half of the vessel.

Along each side of the berthdeck were rooms of different sizes for various uses. One was the powder magazine, one the shell magazine, one was the dispensary where medicines and hospital supplies were kept; one room was for the men's clothes-bags and diddy-bags and boxes, and another for the hammocks. Then there were rooms for the ship's provisions, paymaster's stores, wardroom pantry and storeroom, yeoman's storeman, etc. Beneath the berthdeck was a space about four feet in depth which was divided into stowage-holds for solid shot, grape, cannister, etc., and on one side were three or four tanks for drinking water. This water was condensed from steam in the engine room and pumped forward into the tanks.

An iron bulkhead terminated the berthdeck-space aft, through which opened three bulkhead-doors. The one on the starboard side opened into the galley, that on the port side opened into a passageway leading aft to the fireroom, and that in the centre opened into the turret-chamber, as the space directly beneath the turret was named.

This turret-chamber was a room fifteen feet square, and located there were the two blowers (with small engines to run them) which forced air into the forward part of the vessel. Here, also, was the powerful engine which revolved the turret, and the machinery which moved the tiller ropes. This steering machinery was operated by arms geared to a steel shaft which moved up or down in a slot cut in the large shaft which supported the pilot-house above the turret. Outside the turret-chamber walls were the heavy iron beams and braces which carried the tremendous weight of the turret and guns.

In the galley was the large range on and in which all of the cooking was done. There were three cooks working in the galley; one was the captain's cook, who cooked for the captain, his steward and boy; one was the wardroom cook, who cooked for the ten officers, the ward-room steward, and four boys; the third was the ship's cook, who cooked for the about sixty men of the crew, which consisted of the petty officers, seamen, ordinary seamen, and landsmen, firemen and coalheavers.

The turret was twenty-one feet in diameter and nine feet high. It was built of eleven inches thickness of inch-thick iron plates, their edges over-lapping and all strongly bolted together. Heavy steel beams supported the massive iron gun-carriages on which were mounted the two great guns. These were muzzle-loading, smooth bore, and of the type known as "Dahlgren shell guns".[2] On hooks hanging from the overhead beams were the long-handled rammers, sponges, etc., used in swabbing out and loading the guns. There were two ellipse-shaped portholes, which were about eighteen inches wide by three feet high, cut through the side of the turret, and through these portholes the guns were fired.

The XI-inch gun could be run out so that the muzzle extended a few inches beyond the edge of the turret, but the muzzle of the XV-inch gun was larger than the porthole, hence that gun had to be discharged while inside the turret. A cast-iron flange, the inside diameter of which was an inch larger all around than the bore of the gun, was bolted onto the muzzle. As this flange was beveled to fit up against the inner curve of the turret wall, when the gun was run up to the edge of

---

2. John A. Dahlgren designed an iron shell gun in the 1850s the characteristic feature of which was a thickening at the breech that gave the gun the appearance of a soda bottle. Dahlgren smoothbores were manufactured in nine-, ten-, and eleven-inch calibers. The fifteen-inch model mentioned by Hunter was introduced to the fleet only in late 1862.

the porthole and fired, most of the smoke from the gun passed out through the porthole. As a further protection, a cupboard like space two feet within the turret wall was enclosed with a one-fourth-inch thick iron partition. Through this partition the muzzle of the gun extended, a sliding shutter enclosing the muzzle of the gun at the inner wall of the cupboard.

Obviously the gunner couldn't sight the gun over the top in the usual way, and a sighting apparatus was set in a tiny peephole in the side of the turret three or four feet to the right of the porthole, through which the officer in charge of that gun did the sighting. Orders for elevating the muzzle of the gun, or for turning the turret to right or left so as to bring the gun to bear upon the target, were given by the officer at the peephole.

Ponderous port-stoppers of wrought iron, about ten inches thick and broad enough to completely cover the portholes on the inside, were so pivoted that they could be swung by levers to one side so that the guns could be run out to be fired. As soon as a gun was fired, the stopper was swung back to close the porthole against any shot which might possibly strike there.

The top of the turret was made of railroad-iron beams set about a foot apart, on which were laid half-inch-thick iron plates, which were well perforated with holes an inch in diameter to give ventilation. Wooden gratings were laid down on the turret-top, and this turret-top was the ship's quarter deck when we were at sea, or when the wind was sufficently strong to cause waves to wash over the main deck, which sometimes happened in a broad harbor.

An iron ladder led up from the turret-chamber floor through a small hatchway in the floor of the turret beside the XV-inch gun, and from there a second iron ladder led up through another small hatchway in the top of the turret. These two ladders were movable, and were taken down and stored whenever we went into battle, or when for any purpose the turret was to be revolved. On the outside of the turret was a fixed iron ladder leading down to the main deck. When we were at sea, with all the deck-hatches closed and battened down, to reach the main deck from the berthdeck or wardroom it was necessary to go through the turret-chamber, up the two ladders to the top of the turret, then down the fixed ladder to the deck.

When the turret was to be revolved, it was lifted up a half-inch from the packing in the groove in the deck in which it rested when not in use, an ingenious mechanism having been devised for lifting the huge bulk, guns and all. An engine in the turret-chamber, geared to a huge wheel on the underside of the turret, turned the turret to the right or left as ordered, until the guns bore upon the target. When we went to sea, the turret was let down until it rested upon a firm packing in the groove in the deck, which packing was supposed to exclude the water which was constantly washing over the deck when there was any sea running. As a matter of fact this packing didn't wholly exclude the water, and caulking of the narrow space about the base of the turret was resorted to whenever we were going a distance at sea.

Above the turret, supported on a solid iron shaft twelve inches in diameter, was a circular pilot-house, which was six feet in diameter inside and built of nine thicknesses of inch-thick iron plates, these plates being put on with edges lapping over each other and all strongly bolted together. Inside the pilot-house was the steering wheel, which was ingeniously geared to an inch-square steel rod which was moved up and down in a slot cut into the side of the supporting shaft. This steel rod was again geared to operating arms in the turret-chamber, and those quarter-turn arms communicated the movement to the tiller ropes which extended aft to the rudder head.

There were adequate peep-holes cut through the sides of the pilot-house at convenient distances apart to give the pilot and helmsman a view of things outside, and to give as wide a view as possible the peep-holes were splayed to about six inches diameter on the inside. As the outside diameter of the peep-holes was but one and one-half inches, slots half an inch wide were cut to right and left of each peep-hole, which considerably widened the angle of vision. The top of the pilot-house was of two inch-thick iron plates, slightly domed, and perforated with holes to give ventilation.

Directly aft of the turret-chamber were the boilers, set in the centre of the ship, with cavernous coal bunkers along each side, excepting that about ten feet of space on the starboard side was occupied by the galley and about twenty-five feet of the space on the port side was made into a storeroom for boat davits, oars, awnings, stanchions, etc., and toilet rooms. Next aft of the boilers was the fireroom, where the firemen and coalheavers fed and tended the furnaces beneath the boilers, and the engineers and oilers attended to the engine.

The engine was of unique design, made especially for the monitors, and concentrated into the smallest possible space. One massive cylinder contained the two pistons, which plunged alternately into the cylinder, the steam passing into the cylinder at the middle and operating to push the pistons, first one and then the other, out towards the ends, where they connected with oscillating arms on a small shaft, second arms transmitting the motion by connecting rods to the propeller shaft below the cylinder. The "grasshopper-like" movements of this reciprocating engine attracted me greatly, and after I had made friends with the engineer's storekeeper, a youth named Hatch from Lowell, Massachusetts, who was in charge of a small storeroom located away aft in the stern, I could get many an evening half-hour's enjoyment of it when the engine was running.

Set around the sides of the engine room were various small engines. One of these was a condenser for cooling steam into fresh water, two were pumps for forcing water into the boilers or for pumping out any water which might have found its way into the hold, and there was a fine centrifugal pump, capable of throwing up a geyser-like stream of water five inches in diameter. This last was received aboard and set in place after we sailed for the South. An iron ladder extended from the fireroom floor to a hatchway opening onto the main deck a little way aft of the smokestack, and a ventilating shaft gave fresh air to the heated workers in the fireroom. The fuel was anthracite coal and we had bunker capacity for about two hundred tons.

The main deck of the ship was eight inches thick, of oak timbers resting upon oak beams, and was covered with two thicknesses of inch-thick iron plates strongly bolted down. The deck was very slightly domed, so that water would flow off the sides all around. There were three flagstaffs—one was away forward and another clear aft, and these two were held upright by iron tripods bolted to the deck, the third flagstaff was above the pilot-house.

The deck was cut through in many places—by the three hatchways mentioned, by a small circular hatchway over the anchorwell, a large oblong hatch over the propeller and a small one over the steam-drum just above the engine. Then, there were some two score dead-lights (small circular windows) which gave light to the staterooms, the cabin and wardroom, berthdeck, etc.

These numerous openings through the deck were all closed by iron hatches when we prepared for action. These hatches were two inches thick, made of two inch-thick iron plates, the upper plate extending an inch all around beyond the lower one, the extension forming a flange. The hatches were secured in place by stout bolts passing through iron bars beneath the deck beams, and there were rubber gaskets provided for them which were supposed to prevent water leaking through. Many of the gaskets, however, were defective, so the seams around the important hatches were caulked when we were going to sea.

The circular hatches over the deadlights were only put on when we were going into action, and were secured in place from beneath by hooking a stout hook into an equally stout eyebolt. But we found that the discharge of a gun which was pointing forward over the deck was liable to loosen one or more of these deadlight hatches, after learning which we boys used to tie each hook into its eyebolt with a ropeyarn.

The deadlights were made of circular plates of thick glass enclosed in metal frames, which were hinged on one side and secured in place by a stout thumb-screw at the opposite side. There was a beveled edge around the metal frame of the light, which shut against and into a rubber gasket set into the deadlight frame, and this gasket was supposed to make the deadlight watertight. The deadlight hatches not being put on excepting when we were going into action, the water flowing across the deck when we were at sea, and waves flowing over, caused very curious and interesting lighting effects in the rooms beneath. The water twisted about and boiled in the deadlight-cavity, and, being more or less charged with air bubbles, the constantly changing shades of green light were a pleasure to study.

Each stateroom was equipped with a candle-socket of metal, which hung beside the mirror and was pivoted two ways like a mariner's compass, and a spiral spring set in the base of the socket acted to push up the parafin candle as fast as it burned away at the top. In the wardroom, on the berthdeck and in different dark passages, ship's lanterns were hung. As the globes of these lanterns were of refracting lenses, they supplied a fair amount of light, and the lanterns and candles were our artificial light. In the lanterns whale oil was the fuel burned.

3 ‖ A LONG VOYAGE TO NEW YORK
‖ THE VOYAGE TO FORTRESS
‖ MONROE

THE THREE DAYS OF OUR STAY AT THE CHARLESTOWN NAVY YARD
included New Year's Day of 1863, but we were too busy to consider
such a minor matter. We were doing our best to get away to the South,
where duty called. Early in the afternoon of January 2d, Mr. [Charles
E.] Clark, who was one of our watch officers, lived in Chelsea, and
was well acquainted with my Aunt Hatch, told me he was going over
to Chelsea to bid his family good bye and he would get leave for me if I
cared to go along and make a short call upon my relatives.

This first leave I greatly enjoyed, and the pleasure was the greater
because Cousin Dessie[1] had made a "housewife" for me. This was duly
presented, fully equipped with needles, thread, buttons, scissors, etc.
This useful little companion has travelled many thousands of miles
with me in the more than fifty years that I have owned it, and it is still
fit for duty. That evening I asked for and was given another two-hours'
leave, and made a hurried call upon Aunt Folsom and the cousins in
Charlestown. My recollection of these two visits is that I most enjoyed
showing myself in my sailor's uniform.

The next forenoon all was bustle and confusion in the hurry of
getting endless last things on board and the workmen ashore, and the
work of finishing the cabin and wardroom wasn't really all done when
we cast off from the dock and steamed out into Boston Harbor. A

---

1. Modesta Hatch (called Dessie) was the daughter of William and Sarah Hatch. She
was a few years older than Alvah.

powerful sea-going tugboat had come around from New York to help us along by towing, and about mid-afternoon she got one end of our big hawser made fast and we steamed slowly down the harbor, amid a constant salute from steamers' whistles and ships' bells.

As we drew near to Fort Warren the garrison could be seen marching out upon the rampart, and as we passed out by the fort, three rousing cheers came to us over the water. We answered by blowing the whistle and dipping our flag, and this was our "good bye" to old Boston.

Soon after we passed Fort Warren there came a slight lifting of the forward end of the ship and a wave broke upon the deck, sending all hands of us to the top of the turret or below. The monitors sat very low in the water; when fully supplied with coal, ordnance stores and supplies our deck amidship was but a foot above the level of the water when it was quite calm; with a very slight sea running the waves came over the side and washed across the deck.

It being time to make preparations for supper I went below, and on the berth deck came upon one of the most distressing sights I have ever seen. Some despicable creature had smuggled some liquor into the navy yard and sold a quart or two to a group of our men, and half a dozen of our best sailors were fighting-roaring drunk. The master-at-arms, aided by two or three other petty officers, had got the poor fellows in irons, and to shut off their blasphemy and foul-mouthings they were all "bucked and gagged". One of them was as handsome a man as would be seen in a day's journey, a model seaman, and as he looked up at me from his "trussed up" position on the deck I felt greater sorrow for him than I would have thought it possible to feel for a stranger.

In the wardroom some of the deadlights were leaking, and we boys had to run here and there with buckets and pans to catch the water. In half an hour we had run out into a moderate head sea. The motion of the vessel, aided by the close air below, was too much for me and I succumbed to my first attack of seasickness. During the supper hour I managed to stay on the job, with one or two brief absences, and as soon as the officers had left the table I hastened to the top of the turret to get into the open air.

It was a solid-dark winter night, and the angry seas were hissing across the deck. The heavy bulk of the ship would rise a little on the lift of a wave, then the upper half of the wave swept across the deck like a millrace. Every little while a heavier sea would dash against the base of the turret, the spray dashing high in the air and the wind would fling it in my face. As I listened to the waves hissing across the deck the words of the old sailor on the *Ohio* came to my mind: "You'll go to the bottom in her, youngster that's where you'll all go!"

There was a bright light on our starboard beam which the quartermaster told me was Minot's Light, and the stories I had heard of the disaster which befell the first Minot's Ledge Light came to my mind.[2] What with the depression of seasickness and the dismal forebodings of the old sailor, it is not strange that I felt somewhat homesick. After a little time in the open air I crept down the ladders to the turret-chamber, managed to get to my hammock and turned in "all standing" (i.e. without undressing).

A few hours later I awoke to the fact that our engine had stopped. Cautiously I climbed the ladders to the top of the turret and looked about. There was a dense fog and almost no wind. The tugboat had dropped back to easy hailing distance and the pilot on the tug was talking with our officer of the deck. I overheard the words: "Race Point Light. I think we'd better feel our way into Cape Cod harbor and anchor till daylight." After some discussion this seemed to be agreed upon and we steamed slowly ahead again, a man at the rail sounding with a lead every few minutes. An hour later the anchor was let go, and the *Nahant* swung gently upon the ocean swell. I was congratulating myself upon having found a comfortable place under the lee of the pilot-house when the officer of the deck discovered me. I was ordered to "go below and turn in".

The longest night comes to an end. When "All hands! UP *all* hammocks!" was called, I gladly lashed up my hammock and carried it to the hammock-room door, then crept up the ladders to the top of the turret to find that we were shut in by a fog so thick we could scarcely see beyond the ends of the ship. All day of the 4th of January, that night, and most of the next day, we lay at anchor, but towards night on the 5th the wind veered to the north and the fog soon lifted. The anchor was hoisted, the tugboat passed us the end of the hawser, and we again started on our voyage. We passed Cape Cod light about eight o'clock in the evening, and I remember sufficient geography to picture the Atlantic Ocean as stretching away to the eastward to the coasts of

2. Because Minot's Ledge, six and a half miles south of Boston, had been the scene of numerous shipwrecks, an iron frame lighthouse was erected there between 1847 and 1850. Barely a year later, in April 1851, a strong gale completely destroyed the lighthouse, killing its two resident keepers. A newer, stronger lighthouse was built in 1852.

France and Spain. With the lights of Cape Cod close at hand, however, it did not seem as though we were very far at sea.

Before morning the wind died down and fog shut us in again. Being in comparatively shoal water, we anchored for some hours and had exercise at "Quarters", or battle practice. On board a warship every individual has a station. When "general quarters" is sounded it is the duty of everyone to get to his station at once, and remain there until the recall is sounded.

The boys on a warship are given the duty of passing cartridges from the curtain hanging before the magazine door to the vicinity of the guns—on an old-time man-of-war the boys were called "powder monkeys". Buckets made of heavy leather and having covers of leather were provided to carry the cartridges in, and when the empty buckets were being returned to the magazine door, the cover was lifted, the bucket turned upside down over a tub of water, which had been provided for the purpose, to dump out and drown any scattering grains of powder which might be in them.

As the powder cartridges for our XV-inch gun weighed thirty-five and forty-five pounds each and the leather tubs in which to carry them weighed perhaps twenty pounds each, it was thought that "a boy" was not strong enough to carry both cartridge and tub, so a man was detailed to carry the tub and cartridge to the turret-chamber door, but when the empty tub was handed out to the berth deck again, one of the boys seized it, inverted and shook it over the tub of water, then another boy took it back to the magazine door. By this ingenious arrangement the regulation that everyone must have a station and duty was sustained, although the man who had brought up the tub and cartridge was doing nothing while a boy carried the tub back to the magazine door.

A little after mid-day the fog thinned somewhat, but the barometer was slowly falling, and so, after another consultation, we hove up the anchor and steamed ahead for two or three hours, then turned into the entrance to Narragansett Bay. A little before dark we dropped anchor in the harbor of Newport, Rhode Island. That evening we heard of the sinking of the *Monitor*, which had foundered off Cape Hatteras on the night of December 30–31, when on the way to Port Royal, South Carolina.[3]

3. The *Monitor* sank in a storm off Cape Hatteras in the early morning hours of 30 December 1862. Four officers and twelve men lost their lives when the vessel went to the bottom in 200 feet of water.

The U.S. Naval Academy had been removed from Annapolis, Maryland, to Newport a year or so previous,[4] and the next day after our arrival we remained at anchor there in Newport harbor to give the Midshipmen of the Academy opportunity to inspect one of the new-type warships. Our crew was exercised at quarters and the XV-inch gun was fired for the Middies' instruction.

The morning of January 8th dawned bright and fair. Directly after daylight we got underway and put out to sea. There was some discomfort as we passed Point Judith, but after we entered Long Island Sound the voyage was enjoyable. There was sufficient sea running to cause some motion to the ship and the deck was wet all day, but the bright, mid-winter sun shown down upon us as we steamed slowly along, and those of us green hands who had been seasick felt that possibly "a life on the ocean wave" wasn't all to the bad.

The huge, unwieldly bulk of the *Nahant*, together with her sitting so low in the water, made steering her a decidedly difficult task. She would swing off to starboard or port in spite of the best efforts of the helmsman to "meet her", and our progress was so slow that all of that day and night were consumed in the voyage down the Sound. About seven o'clock in the morning of January 9th we passed through Hell Gate, and about eight-thirty o'clock we made fast to a dock in the Brooklyn naval yard, five and a half days from Boston to New York.

For a week we lay at the Brooklyn Navy Yard, having some added machinery put in, taking in stores, coal, etc., and without important incidents excepting when we cast off from the dock one day to pull out into the stream a bit, so as to escape the attentions of the swarm of visitors that constantly annoyed us. There was a swift tide running at the time, and decidedly lively half-hour we had before the ship was got under control and made fast to another dock.

On the 12th of January there came aboard and reported for duty Pilot Isaac Sofield, who proved to be an important addition to our group of officers. He had been captain of a coasting schooner hailing from New Jersey, had just passed an examination for a commission as pilot, and upon receiving his commission had been ordered to the *Nahant*. As he was a competent officer, he was, at his own suggestion, given regular watch duty on deck, thus giving us four watch-officers

4. The U.S. Naval Academy at Annapolis was moved to the Atlantic House Hotel in Newport, Rhode Island, in April 1861. The vacated buildings at Annapolis became an army post and field hospital. The Academy moved back to Annapolis in the summer of 1865.

and one of the four would have an "all-night-in" every night. There
being no stateroom for an extra officer, a cot-bed was slung for him at
night above one end of the wardroom table, and he used for a dressing
room the stateroom of the watch officer who was on duty.

On the afternoon of January 16th we left the Brooklyn Navy Yard
and steamed down the harbor to just inside Sandy Hook, where we
anchored and spent a day in tests for variation in our ship's compass.
Where there is so great a mass of iron as a monitor consisted of, the
compass was influenced by it, and it was necessary that the variations
of the needle should be studied. To negative so far as possible the "pull"
of the mass of iron, the compass was elevated about six feet above the
top of the pilot-house, and it was enclosed in a copper shaft which was
much like the common stove-pipe. A mirror hung in a pivoted frame
just in front of the man who stood at the wheel, and by adjusting this
mirror at the proper angle, the position of the needle could be noted.

In the afternoon of January 18th we hove up anchor, passed the
end of our towing hawser to the tugboat again, steamed out to sea and
turned south. It was a bright mid-winter day, and we steamed along
within two or three miles of the coast of New Jersey, which was in
plain view all the afternoon. There was so little sea running, the crew
was called to quarters and exercised at battle practice for an hour. By
the next morning, however, a change had come over the sky, the
barometer was falling steadily, and after a consultation between the
pilot on the tugboat and Captain Downes, it was decided that we turn
into the entrance to Delaware Bay and anchor behind the breakwater.

The wind steadily increased to a moderate gale, then a heavy gale,
and during the next day two or three score vessels of various kinds ran
in and anchored behind the breakwater. One of these was an army
transport with a load of wounded soldiers. This steamer sent a boat to
us to tell that they were short of bread and we supplied them with two
hundred pounds of ship's bread. The gale was very heavy, accompanied
by a driving rain, and for three days we were stormbound, witnessing
the distress of several vessels which dragged their anchors in spite of
the protection afforded by the breakwater, and all of us green hands
were wretchedly seasick. Tremendously heavy swells rolled into the
harbor around the south end of the breakwater and poured over the
top of that substantial barrier.

So heavy was the ground-swell within the harbor, our anchor had
great difficulty in holding, and we veered chain until we had let out
practically all we had in the lockers. When the storm passed on, during

the 23d, four or five schooners were high and dry on the beach back of the harbor, and our crew had a hard task getting in the great length of chain we had out. The propeller was kept turning to ease the pull upon the chain, the men worked in double-shift, and it was more than two hours before word was passed that the anchor had broken ground. Just before dark the tugboat took us in tow again and we stood out to sea. Late the next afternoon, we passed in between the Virginia capes and about eight o'clock in the evening we came to anchor in Hampton Roads, but a short distance from the famous Fortress Monroe.[5]

The next day, Sunday, January 25th, we hoisted our anchor and steamed up into the mouth of the James River, coming to anchor about a mile off Newport News and close to the scene of the great fight between the *Monitor* and *Merrimack*. Near at hand the tops of the masts of the frigate *Cumberland* could be seen sticking up out of the water. The *Cumberland* had been rammed and sunk by the *Merrimack* in the first day's battle, the day before the *Monitor* had arrived upon the scene.[6]

There were rumors of there being another Confederate ram up the James River, and being about to come down to attack our fleet of wooden vessels, hence the policy of the Navy Department of having the new monitors report at Hampton Roads, and two of these monitors were kept stationed off Newport News to protect our fleet. Whenever a new monitor arrived at this station, she released the one longest on duty there, and that one departed for Port Royal, South Carolina, where a fleet of ironclad vessels was being assembled for an intended attack upon Charleston. The arrival of the *Nahant* at Hampton Roads released the *Patapsco*, which sailed the next day for Port Royal.

The monitors had no fixed railing round the deck, but iron stanchions about two and a half feet high were set in holes eight or ten feet apart around the outer edge of the deck, and two stout ropes were run through eye-holes in those stanchions, one eye-hole being at the top and the others about a foot down from the top; these stanchions

5. Built in the 1820s and 30s, Fort Monroe was a large masonry fort at the tip of the Virginia peninsula formed by the York and James rivers. It commanded the waters of Hampton Roads and remained in Union hands even after the secession of Virginia.

6. The first sortie of the C.S.S. *Virginia (Merrimack)* on 8 March 1862 resulted in the destruction of two U.S. Navy steam frigates—the *Cumberland*, which was rammed and sunk, and the *Congress*, which ran itself aground to avoid the same fate. The *Monitor* arrived in Hampton Roads the next day.

and ropes served the purpose of a railing, and were quickly taken down and stored below when the deck was cleared for action. On each side of the deck just a little aft of the turret stood two heavy ironboat davits, from the tackles of which hung the two large ship's boats known as the 1st and 2d cutters; in one of these large boats the captain's gig was housed when we went to sea.

"Clearing the deck for action" consisted in taking down and stowing below the boat davits, the railing stanchions and ropes, the galley smokepipe which stood just beside the turret, and everything which might be in the way of shots from the guns. All the hatches were put on, and they were secured in place from beneath, and when the deck was cleared for action the ship was stripped to her smooth iron armor; she was wholly free from all obstruction to fighting, and the guns could be brought to bear upon any point of the horizon excepting the half-dozen feet just back of the turret where stood the smokestack. This small space directly astern we could not reach without the ship being turned a few feet to starboard or port.

For three weeks we remained in Hampton Roads, working the crew into shape by daily exercise at quarters, by two or three day's practice firing at a target, by revolver practice, exercise with single-sticks, etc. What came near to being a serious accident occurred while firing the XV-inch gun. The cast-iron flange bolted to the muzzle of this gun was broken away by the force of the explosion. The force was so great as to throw up the top-armor of the turret, which simply rested upon the railroad-iron beams, and the iron ladder, which had been drawn up from the turret and lay on the gratings, was thrown clear over the side of the ship and lost. Fortunately none of the gun crew were standing near the muzzle, and no one was severely hurt.

The mild winter weather of that part of Virginia was greatly enjoyed by everyone. On both the Sundays that we spent there, muster and inspection of the crew was held on deck, followed by inspection of the ship by Captain Downes accompanied by Mr. Harmony, and then there was the reading of the church service by Doctor Stedman, acting as Chaplain.

A welcome addition to our table fare was the fine oysters of the region, and fresh fish in abundance could be bought from the fishermen who came alongside in boats to sell to our stewards. A few days before we left Hampton Roads, a raft was noticed floating past towards the sea, with what looked to be a fishing seine lying on it. One of the boats put off in pursuit of the raft, and not only was a pretty good seine found on it, but a pair of oyster tongs also. Both of these "finds" were sources of much pleasure to our crew when we were in South Carolina and Georgia waters, and they also added materially to our supply of eatables.

Our stores of all kinds were replenished, the coal bunkers were filled to capacity, and on Monday, February 16th, we sailed for Port Royal, South Carolina.

4 ‖ THE VOYAGE TO PORT ROYAL

‖ THE FIGHTING AT FORT McALLISTER

WE LEFT OUR ANCHORAGE OFF NEWPORT NEWS, VIRGINIA, a little after noon on February 16th, and steamed down past Fortress Monroe before the gunboat *State of Georgia* took us in tow. About dark we passed Cape Henry and stood south, butting into a heavy head sea and the ship laboring heavily.

The next two days and nights were so many hours of most abject misery to me; each hour seemed endless. About mid-afternoon of the 18th as I was lying in a fold of the turret awning, which was rolled up and hanging from the stanchions set about the edge of the turret-top, the thick clouds, which were flying low, opened up for a few minutes as we were off Cape Hatteras. I got upon my shaky legs for a few seconds and was rewarded by a glimpse of the distant Cape Hatteras Light before the clouds shut down again. We were then near the spot where the *Monitor* had foundered.

All of those two days and nights that the heavy seas were sweeping over our decks one of the men, clad in oilskins, stood by a boat davit, (to which he was securely lashed), and hove the lead at about fifteen-minute intervals; the leadsman was relieved every hour.

Early on the morning of the 19th, before it was fairly light, I had crept up the ladders to the top of the turret so as to get into the open air, when one of the sailors began having fun at my expense and urged that I take a hearty drink of sea water to relieve my seasickness. After enduring his jibes for a while I told him to fetch me a pot of sea water and I'd drink it. He went below and got a quart pot, then went down the ladder on the outside of the turret till he could dip up water from a sea that swept across the deck; he brought the pot to me nearly full, and said: "There, youngster, take a good swig of that and you'll be all right."

I put the pot to my lips and drank and drank. The water was cool and refreshing, and did not taste so very salt. In a few minutes I began to feel better and my head began to clear. Within fifteen minutes I went down the ladders to the berthdeck and wardroom, and assisted in preparing the table for breakfast. After the officers had eaten, we boys sat down and ate, and it is safe to state that no meal ever tasted better to me than the breakfast I ate that morning.

About mid-forenoon I had an adventure which might have been disastrous. It was desired to communicate with the *State of Georgia* by signals, the desire being made known to the officers on the gunboat by our setting a signal pennant at the top of the flagstaff on our bow, the signalling flags which conveyed the message being raised and lowered on the flagstaff above our pilot-house. When the signalling had been completed, it was necessary that the pennant on the forward flagstaff should come down, and I asked the old quartermaster to let me run forward and haul it down. There was a line rove along the middle of the deck, from the turret forward through several stanchions to the three-legged stand which supported the flagstaff; this line was a new one-inch Manilla rope.

The seas seemed to be quite moderate just at the time, and I got forward to the flagstaff and got the pennant down all right, keeping one leg hooked over one of the legs of the flagstaff-stand so as to have both hands free. Gathering the pennant into one hand, I turned to start back to the turret. At that moment I felt the deck lifting, and before I had got three steps from the bow a great green wave came dashing over the side upon the deck. A shout to "look out" came from the officer of the deck on top of the turret, but the warning wasn't necessary. I grasped the life-line with my right hand before the crest of the wave struck me, and when it came I was swept from my feet instantly. The force of the wave was so great I was straightened right out on and *in* the water.

In three or four seconds the bulk of the wave had gone past and I got my feet down to the deck again, but it was several seconds later before I could relax my fingers sufficiently to let go the line. When I had reached the top of the turret and handed the signalling pennant to the quartermaster, I found there were two or three tiny fibres of the Manilla rope embedded in the skin of my right hand.

On the morning of February 20th we passed the lightship off Port Royal, and about noon we reached the anchorage of the naval vessels in that spacious harbor. Port Royal, South Carolina, was bombarded and captured by the fleet under the command of Admiral Du Pont, in November, 1861, and immediately became the repair and relief station of the South Atlantic Blockading Squadron and the headquarters of the army operating in that department. The army headquarters were located at Hilton Head, a large island on the southern side of the entrance, and the naval anchorage was perhaps two miles up the harbor.[1]

In the more than a year during which Port Royal had been occupied by the army and navy, Hilton Head had grown to be a considerable town, with wharves, many stores and dwellings, and the upper half of the harbor had developed into a naval repair and supply station of great value to the fleet blockading the southern ports. A machine shop had been made out of two large hulks which had been drawn up onto the shore and placed side by side, and there were adequate shears for hoisting heavy machinery, etc.

A weekly mail steamer from the North came and went, army transports and supply steamers were coming in and going out almost daily, and naval vessels were regularly coming for repairs, coal, etc. These naval vessels would spend two or three days or a week in port, then depart to one or another of the blockading stations up or down the coast. What with these and the fleets of coal schooners and supply vessels of various kinds coming and going, Port Royal in 1863–4 was one of the busiest harbors on the Atlantic seaboard.

The old Line-of-battle-ship *Vermont* was anchored a little to one side of the naval anchorage, and was used as a receiving and hospital ship. Another old ship, the *Valparaiso*, was a department store on a small scale, being stocked with many kinds of goods to eat, drink or

1. A Federal fleet under the command of Flag Officer Samuel F. Du Pont seized Port Royal, South Carolina, on 7 November 1861. Union warships quickly battered the two Confederate forts into submission and took possession of the spacious waters of Port Royal Sound. This was significant not only because it provided an important base of operations for the Union blockading fleet, but also because it seemed to demonstrate the superiority of naval gunfire to shore fortifications. The Confederate forts, however, were hastily erected earthworks and far inferior to the powerful fortresses guarding Charleston.

wear. The drinkables, however, were non-intoxicating, were what would now be called "soft drinks", since all alcoholic beverages had been banished from the vessels of the United States Navy by a regulation which went into effect some months previous.[2]

In addition to this naval storeship, there were good stores at Hilton head, which was within easy reach, and about once in three weeks the vessels of the blockading fleet were visited by a regular supply steamer, the *Massachusetts*, which came down the coast with a load of fresh meats, vegetables, fruits, etc., and in summer ice in moderate supply was brought down and distributed among the vessels on blockade and in the harbor.

The mild, spring-like days of that southern climate were greatly enjoyed by officers and men alike. Small flatboats or dugout canoes, each having a darkey man and woman aboard, would come alongside to solicit laundry work from the officers, and these darkey visitors would also bring alongside a few eggs, a pair of fowls, or a basket of fresh fish, to sell. The crew was given a washday once a week, when there was abundant opportunity to wash and dry clothes.

Encouraged by the good weather, the men got out their diddy-bags and boxes, bought blue cloth or flannel, sewing silk, etc. of the purser, and employed their spare hours in cutting and making shirts and trousers. Inspired by the good example, I bought some blue flannel, black sewing silk, etc., got out my "housewife", and cut and made for myself a flannel shirt, working fancy stars on the collar and a crowsfoot at the bottom of the neck opening. Of this piece of domestic handiwork I was no-end proud when I showed it to friends after my return home.

One of the greatest comforts which now came to us were coamings for the hatchways and windsails for the deadlights. These were bolted to the deck about the openings, had rubber gaskets under the edges to make them watertight, and could be kept on all the time that we were not in a seaway. These hatch coamings and windsails were made of copper, the coamings being about a foot and a half high, (low enough to be stepped over), and the windsails were about five feet tall. These last had bonnet-like tops which could be turned to face the wind to conduct the air below, or away from the wind when rain was falling.

2. For centuries, one of the perquisites of enlisted life on a man-of-war was the daily ration of grog—a mixture of rum and water. In the U.S. Navy, the traditional daily grog ration of half-a-gill per sailor was terminated in 1862 and as compensation sailors pay was raised slightly.

These coamings and windsails gave us good ventilation day and night, and added much to the comfort of all hands.

Eight busy days went by, the crew having daily exercise at the guns or busy taking in coal and supplies, and on Sunday, March 1st, in the company of the monitors *Passaic* and *Patapsco* towed by steamers, we put out to sea in tow of the gunboat *Flambeau* and again headed south.[3] In the afternoon we arrived off Ossabaw Sound, Georgia, received a local pilot, steamed in over the bar, across the sound and up the Great Ogeechee River several miles.

Admiral Du Pont had thought it wise to give the monitors something of "a try-out" under fire before they should go into the approaching fight with Fort Sumter, for which purpose the ironclad ships were being assembled at Port Royal. The monitor *Montauk* had been sent to the Great Ogeechee sometime before we went down there, with orders to attempt the reduction of an earthwork known as Fort McAllister, and, if possible, to destroy the Confederate steamer *Nashville*, which had run the blackade into the Ogeechee, had been outfitted for a privateer and was now waiting for an opportunity to escape to sea.

Captain [John L.] Worden, who had commanded the *Monitor* in the famous fight with the *Merrimack* in Hampton Roads, was now in command of the *Montauk*, and was standing on the deck of that vessel as we steamed slowly past her. Captain Worden and Captain Downes were warm friends, and the boy-like enthusiasm of the former was very manifest as he called across the narrow space between the two vessels and told Captain Downes of his having effected the complete destruction of the *Nashville* the day before. Captain Worden fairly danced up and down with enthusiasm as he told of the jolly-good-time he had enjoyed!

When the *Montauk* had come up the Great Ogeechee she had reconnoitered up river till Captain Worden discovered a line of strong piles set across the channel of the river a little below the fort, and there were indications of torpedoes below (but near) the row of obstructions. On two different days he had steamed up river and shelled the fort for some hours each, being supported by four small wooden gunboats which had thrown shells from their rifled guns from long-

3. The *Passaic* and *Patapsco* were sister ships of the *Nahant*. The *Flambeau* was a small screw steamer mounting two rifled guns and frequently used to tow the lubberly monitors in open water.

A Union ironclad monitor fires on Fort McAllister in the Ogeechee River while Union steam frigates look on. This drawing is from a sketch by a Union naval officer. (U.S. Navy)

range distance. On one of these days the *Montauk* had steamed up to within six hundred yards of the fort. On one day she had been struck thirteen times and on the other forty-six times, without sustaining any injury worth mentioning.

Late in the afternoon of February 27th, Captain Worden discovered the *Nashville* in motion up river, a mile or so above Fort McAllister, and after watching her for a time he became convinced that she had run aground in a bend of the river, and in a position which was within range of his guns if he could bring his ship up to the position near the fort which she had reached two or three days before. At daylight the next morning the *Montauk* steamed up to the desired position, anchored, and began firing shells across the intervening marsh at the *Nashville*. Within twenty minutes she was on fire forward, amidship and aft! Within an hour from the time she was on fire she had burned to the water's edge.

Of course the garrison of the fort had not been idle during this time, but they seemed to be greatly excited and most of their shots went wild. They scored but five hits on the *Montauk*, which calmly withdrew down river as soon as it was certain the work of destruction was complete. The wrecked machinery of the *Nashville* could be plainly seen, perhaps two miles distant over the marsh, as we steamed slowly past the *Montauk* and dropped our anchor a little way above.[4]

The next day we cleared the deck for action, then covered the entire deck with about an eighth of an inch depth of filthy grease called "slush" upon the theory that with our nearly level deck covered with grease, any shot striking it would more readily glance off, and there would be less danger of the deck being penetrated by the shot.

On the morning of March 3d the monitors *Passaic*, *Patapsco* and *Nahant* steamed up river to within convenient range of the fort, the first about twelve, the second fifteen, and the third eighteen hundred yards distant. At 8.40 the Confederates opened fire upon the leading ship, and at 8.45 we dropped our anchor and began a return fire, using shells in both guns.

The carriage of our XV-inch gun acted badly from the first. The compressor, which acted to clamp the guides of the carriage down upon the steel beams upon which the carriage rested, would not work right, and at each discharge the recoil of that gun was more and more vicious. At the twentieth discharge the rivets which secured the guides to the carriage broke entirely away, the loosened guides falling through to the turret-chamber below. This accident didn't wholly disable the gun and a few more shells were fired from it, but the shooting was extra-hazardous because the gun was likely to recoil by successive jumps, instead of sliding smoothly along the beams.

Our firing was extremely slow. It took five full minutes, and from that to six or eight minutes, to load and fire our XV-inch gun, and about three minutes to load and fire the Xl-inch gun. The guns were muzzle loading, and the rammer and sponge handles were stout poles

---

4. Worden's success in destroying the *Nashville* added to the luster he had earned while in command of the *Monitor* in its engagement with the *Virginia (Merrimack)*. After the war he was promoted to Rear Admiral and served as superintendent of the U.S. Naval Academy (1869–74) and as commander of the European squadron (1875–77). The drill field at Annapolis is named for him.

about fifteen feet long each, hence could not be handled quickly and easily in the narrow spaces inside the turret alongside the guns.

When a gun was discharged, the recoil brought it well back within the turret, the port stopper was swung around to close the porthole and the turret was turned a third to half-way around so that the portholes were away from the enemy. The port stopper was then swung back and the sponge handle was passed out through the porthole until the sponge could be entered into the muzzle of the gun, then the two men, standing one each side of the muzzle, pushed the sponge down inside the gun till the bottom of the bore was reached; a couple of turns of the sponge and then it was withdrawn. The sponge was like the rammer excepting that the sponge-head was shaped to fit into the concave bore of the gun at the breach, and the head was covered with sheepskin having the wool on. The wool was for wiping out the bore of the gun and catching any sparks which might be left in the gun from the cloth bag which had contained the powder.

Another cartridge-bag of powder had been passed up from below as soon as the gun was fired, and was now placed in the muzzle of the gun and rammed home. The rammer handle had to be passed out through the porthole before the rammer-head could be inserted into the gun, and the handle had to be passed out through the porthole again in withdrawing the rammer from the gun. Next, a shell was rolled along to near the muzzle of the gun, where a grappling-tongs was clasped onto it and a tackle hoisted it to the muzzle; the men pushed it into the muzzle and the rammer was used a second time in ramming the shell home.

There were three time-fuses screwed into holes drilled into the top of the shell, each fuse being capped with a small bit of lead on which was stamped figures which told the number of seconds required for that fuse to burn down to the powder-charge within the shell. If we were ten, twelve or fifteen seconds distant from the target, the fuse-cap so stamped was torn off as the shell was passed into the gun. If we chanced to be within close range, so that the shortest-timed fuse was used, all three fuse-caps were born off, then, in case the short-timed fuse failed to explore the exploding charge there were two more chances that the shell would explore.

A sharp-pointed steel rod was passed down the touchhole of the gun till the cloth envelope of the cartridge was pierced, then it was withdrawn and a primer having a percussion-cap-head was set into the hole. The gun was run out, and the compressor tightly screwed down against the steel beams on which the gun carriage rested, then the turret was turned until the gun bore upon the target. The right elevation of the muzzle of the gun was obtained by turning a huge screw set in an extension of the breach. A lock, much like a small hammer, was fixed near the touchhole, the hammer being swung over and down upon the primer by a sharp pull upon a lanyard attached to it, the gunner holding the lanyard and awaiting the word. When all was ready he gave the word, "All ready, Sir," and the officer in charge of the gun gave the order, "Fire!"

About noon the order to cease firing was passed, the berthdeck hatch was lifted off to air out 'tweendecks, and those of us who cared to went up on deck to see what was to be seen. The *Nahant* had not been struck by a shot, although one small rifled gun on the fort seemed to be paying special attention to us while I was on deck. During that time two shots from that gun passed over our heads and landed with a "chuck" into the marsh beyond.

The first shot I did not notice till it had passed over. One of the sailors pointed out to me the location of that especial gun, and I watched for the next shot. In two or three minutes I saw the muzzle of the gun appear above the rampart and after a few seconds a puff of smoke burst out, then the shot could be seen as distinctly as though it was a batted ball coming towards us. Then came the boom of the gun and the scream of the shot passing through the air, growing more and more shrill as it came nearer, then on to the "chuck" into the marsh.

We boys were called below to help in preparing a lunch for the officers, and while we were busy with the steward, preparing sandwiches, etc., the thought came to me: "How good a cup of hot coffee would taste to them." The galley smokepipe was down, so there was no possibility of coffee being made there, and then the thought came: "Why not do it camp-style!"

I went aft to the fireroom and asked Mr. Bordley, the engineer on duty there, if I could have a shovelful of coal from one of the furnaces to make a pot of coffee on. He was amused at the idea, but put the question up to Mr. Lovering, the chief engineer, who at once said he thought the idea a good one. Back I went to the pantry, fitted up the big coffeepot with the necessary newly-ground coffee, then back to the fireroom to prepare it on the hot coal and when the sandwiches were being passed around to the officers I had the satisfaction of appearing with a tray of hot coffee. These were greeted with warm praise, quite all the praise commissioned officers could rightly bestow upon a boy.

It certainly was an odd experience, preparing and eating a lunch in the midst of our first fight, if we could rightly call so one-sided an affair a fight. The *Nahant* was not struck once that day, and the freely expressed disgust of some of the men, at having taken so great pains to cover the deck with slush and then not being treated to one shot, was most amusing.

About 3.30 o'clock in the afternoon, the saddle in which rested our XI-inch gun became cracked clear across, at the 39th discharge, and that gun was then useless. Just at this time a signal was run up on the *Passaic*, (the captain of the *Passaic* [Captain Daniel Ammen] was the senior officer present, hence in command) to cease firing and withdraw. Our anchor was hoisted and we steamed down river to our former anchorage.

Three mortar schooners, each having a ten or eleven-inch mortar mounted on deck amidship, had been assisting in the attack by throwing their huge shells high in air, to circle over and down or just behind the parapet of the fort. By the aid of a glass it could be seen that great excavations were made in the earth walls of the fort by the exploding shells, and two of the seven guns in it that morning were dismounted during the day, but no serious damage had been done to the fort itself. The shells buried themselves in the earth-walls, and when they exploded a ton or so earth was thrown up, only to fall back into excavations made by previous shells. At the close of the day Fort McAllister was practically as strong as ever.[5]

The *Passaic*, the monitor nearest the fort, received most of the attention paid to us by the enemy. She was struck thirty-four times on various parts of her armor, none of the shots doing damage excepting some that struck on her deck, which was considerably dented and grooved. One ten-inch mortar shell, made extra heavy by being filled with sand, struck the deck of the *Passaic* over one of the beams. Quite a hole was opened in the iron deck and the planking was broken through, and this shell would probably have passed entirely through the deck but for the resistance given by the beam.

During the succeeding two days, we lay at anchor in the river, the men hard at work scraping off the slush which covered the deck. Much "growling" was indulged in because of this manifestly unnecessary work, and at the dirty condition into which the slush had put both ship

5. Fort McAllister remained a Confederate stronghold until it was captured from the landward side in December 1864 by elements of William Tecumseh Sherman's army following its "march to the sea."

and crew. When walking about the deck (most walking was really sliding), the soles of our shoes would become thickly coated with the filthy grease, which was then carried to everything which our shoes touched. The ladders were covered with it, and it was inevitable that more or less of it would get onto our clothing as we passed up and down. Fortunately for us boys, little of it got into the wardroom, so we had but a moderate task of scraping and scrubbing to clean up there.

On the morning of March 6th, we got underway and steamed out of the river, but our boilers "foamed" so badly we anchored in the sound for a couple of hours. About nine o'clock we steamed out over the bar, the steamer *Ericsson* took us in tow, and at about 4:30 that afternoon we again dropped anchor near the flagship in Port Royal Harbor.

5 ‖ Repairing Damages
‖ Fishing and Other Recreations

W<small>E ARRIVED AT PORT ROYAL ON SATURDAY AFTERNOON, AND</small>
Sunday was a much needed day of rest. The crew was mustered for
inspection and reading of the church service, after which our time was
given to letters which had awaited our return and to writing letters
which told friends at home of our first experience under fire. Sunday
was a perfect day, which we greatly enjoyed after our discomforts of
the preceding week. With both of our guns useless, the *Nahant* could
hardly be called a fighting ship, but there was gratification in the
thought that the damage was due to imperfections in the gun carriages
and was not caused by an enemy's shots; repairing the damages was the
first thing to think about.

Monday morning we got underway and steamed up into "Station
Creek", which was near to the naval machine shop and a most convenient anchorage. Station Creek was one of several estuaries opening
into Port Royal harbor, and such as are common in many harbors on
the Atlantic coast. It was not sufficiently broad to permit of a vessel's
anchoring and swinging about at each turn of the tide, but when we
were anchored by both bow and stern, there was sufficient room for a
lighter from the machine shop, or a coal schooner, to come alongside
for necessary attentions, and at high tide a vessel could pass by to an
anchorage above or pass out by us into the harbor.

Mechanics from the machine shop were brought to us on a tugboat each morning and worked upon the XV-inch gun carriage during
the day, the tug coming back for them at night. A lighter from the

machine shop came alongside and hoisted out the cracked (practically broken) saddle of the XI-inch gun, and a few days later brought and hoisted into place a new saddle. Setting out the broken saddle was a strenuous task. Part of the top of the turret had to be lifted off, then stout iron beams, capable of holding up the heavy gun till the new saddle was put in place, had to be got ready, then the gun was hoisted up and secured to the beams by adequate lashings, then the saddle could be hoisted out.

This "saddle" was made necessary by the XI-inch gun being mounted on a carriage intended for a XV-inch gun, the saddle was to reduce the trunnion bearings to the right size for the smaller gun. The saddles first provided for this purpose were of cast iron, and there wasn't sufficient cohesion to the metal to stand the strain put upon it. The new saddles were made of bronze and proved adequate to the strain. The operation of hoisting up the gun, getting out the old saddle and putting in the new one, then lowering the gun back into place, consumed a full week.

Directly after this return to Port Royal, there broke out an epidemic of insubordination among the crew which made sharp discipline necessary, and the order to the master-at-arms to put irons upon this or that offender and consign him to a coal bunker was frequently heard. My diary records only the cases which immediately affected the wardroom boys, and the first mention was on the day we moved into Station Creek. George Patterson and the captain's boy (Jerome Harris, also a colored boy) got to fighting and were put into double irons and sent to a coal bunker. The next day the irons were taken off and the two boys ordered to shake hands, then both were put back on duty. Before that night, however, another wardroom boy, Barney Doyle, was found to be neglecting his duties after having previously been reprimanded for that fault; he was handcuffed and sent aft to a coal bunker.

On large warships there is a regular prison-room called "the brig", but on small vessels no such room is provided, and we, having no "brig", had no convenient place for punishing delinquents other than a coal bunker. An offender was put in double-irons if his offence was decidedly bad, that is, handcuffs were put upon his wrists and similar irons upon his ankles. For minor offences handcuffs only were used, and the culprit was then said to be in single irons. Having one of the wardroom boys undergoing punishment was a hardship for the others, since two of us then had to do the work of three; also one boy had to take aft to the fireroom meals for the boy in a bunker.

One direct result of this outbreak of insubordination was my assuming full charge of a duty which was easy for me, but which had proved decidedly hard for Barney Doyle when it was his turn. This duty was taking a cup of hot coffee and slice of bread and butter to the officer of the deck on morning watch—on duty from four to eight o'clock in the morning. Being naturally an early riser, I was always up and dressed before the getting-up call in the morning, and being up I was at hand to carry the bit of refreshment to the officer of the deck. Poor Barney, however, could never get himself awake until he was aroused by the call: "All hands, *up all* hammocks!" The high-pitched "up" and long-drawn-out "all" of this getting-up call would awaken anyone not absolutely dead with sleep.

Having become decidedly fond of an early "nip" of hot coffee myself, and "standing-in" with the wardroom cook, hence able to get a cup of coffee and half-slice of bread and butter after returning to the galley with the tray, I was rather glad to take on Barney's share of the early-morning duty; and the cup of coffee wasn't the only reward which came to me for my early rising, as an experience of some three months later will show. Our wardroom cook was about the "plainest" negro that I have ever met, and, like most negroes, he had no love for an Irish boy, which Barney certainly was; but I was just plain Yankee, and cook and I had no frictions.

While the repairs to the gun carriage were going on, we boys had discovered that there was particularly good fishing there in Station Creek, and almost every day we spent an hour or two at that sport. Whiting and Mullet in abundance came to our bait, and we had those attractive fish served on the wardroom table about every day.

We were anchored in about twenty-five feet depth of water, hence no great length of fishing line was necessary. A piece of stout wire about fifteen inches long, with a small loop at each end and another in the middle, gave opportunity for three hooks on the line at once. Snells about ten inches long were attached to each end-loop, and the fishline, which was made fast to the middle loop and extended down some fifteen inches below it, carried the third hook. With this three-hook fishing tackle we would now and then haul up two fish at once, and on rare occasions we would draw up three fish at once. These fish weighed about a quarter-pound to a third of a pound apiece, and were very good eating when cooked soon after they were caught.

Crab fishing was another of our sports at this time. Getting an iron hoop from a beef or pork barrel we would make a net by stretching stout fishline or marline across it, making a net of about one-inch mesh, with all crossings of the line securely knotted; about four fathoms of a discarded lead line, attached to the hoop by a tripod-shaped arrangement of lines which would hold the net level, was the fishing line, and a half-pound chunk of beef or pork was the bait.

The bait was securely tied onto the middle of the net, then the net was lowered to the bottom and left there. In from five to ten minutes, the net would be cautiously drawn up, and there would usually be three or four to half-a-dozen crabs holding onto the bait. If the net was drawn up very carefully, the crabs wouldn't become alarmed for their safety till it approached the top of the water, then it could be quickly swished onto the deck before they could escape. On one of our most successful days, with two such nets in operation, we would catch over a bushel of crabs, and it was a poor hour's fishing that didn't reward us with a peck or more. These crabs were promptly boiled in one of the galley coppers, and much good eating was the result.

It was during the fine spring weather of this period that we began to have most enjoyable singing by the crew. The second dog watch, the time from six to eight o'clock in the evening, is the sailor's special recreation time, when there is complete rest from work. The crew would group just abaft the turret on the main deck, with half-a-dozen of the best singers in the centre, and song after song would be called for until eight bells struck.

Almost all of the crew were Massachusetts men, many of them being from the Gloucester and Marblehead fishing fleets, and a fine lot of sailors they were. One of them, a remarkably handsome sailor named Spofford, had a rich baritone voice, and I greatly enjoyed one of his songs, two lines of the chorus of which were:

Hi, Yi,—You ought to see us kitin',
Three fast men all on the road to Brighton.

The "three fast men" were supposed to be enjoying a drive out the famed Brighton Road, and three or four of the crew would be imitating the actions and excitement of drivers of horses which were going at a fast clip, as the chorus was being roared out by twenty or thirty lusty voices. Those evening sings in the open air were highly enjoyed, not only by all on board the *Nahant*, but by the officers and men of other vessels within hearing.

A supply steamer regularly visited the South Atlantic Squadron with fresh provisions, ice, etc., and as we had no method of preserving fresh meats and vegetables, or keeping ice, it was decided to build a large ice box and place it on the main deck aft, where it would not interfere with the range of the guns. This ice box was eight feet long by four feet broad and deep, and when the supply steamer came in, we would buy and stow in it about half a ton of ice, which gave the cabin and wardroom tables cooled water for drinking and enabled us to keep fresh meats, etc., for a week or ten days. The ice was paid for out of the officers' mess fund.

The supply steamer *Massachusetts* came in while we were anchored in Station Creek, and we secured from her 270 pounds of fresh beef and two barrels of potatoes. Nine-tenths of such fresh provisions was cooked for the messes of the crew, but one or two good roasts of beef and sundry steaks went to the cabin and wardroom tables. The men greatly enjoyed having boiled beef and potatoes, or a hot, nourishing stew, for dinner, also a nice pan of beef and potato "scouse"[1] for breakfast, for several days after the coming in of the supply steamer.

Each mess on the berthdeck had one member who was the "cook" for that mess; not that he cooked anything, all of the cooking for the crew was by the ship's cook in the galley. Each mess-cook had charge of the dishes and food of his mess. He got out and spread on the berth deck the mess-cloth, which was a sheet of canvas about six feet square, painted, a little before each meal time. He set out the tin plates and cups, knives, spoons, etc., got out the pan of ship's bread (hard tack), and at the call went to the galley door and drew the tin bucketful of boiling-hot water which became tea or coffee for the meal. The dry coffee or tea, together with the sugar for sweetening, was put into the bucket before it was taken to the galley door, the hot water was drawn into the bucket, the cover clapped on, and in a few minutes the tea or coffee was ready to serve.

The ship's cook was a short and stout Irishman,[2] with a round, jovial face, and was said to have worked in the kitchen of a well-known Boston hotel. He spoke with quite a bit of brogue, and when he stepped out of the galley, drew himself up to his full height and called: "Dhaaw yer tay wather, cooooks!" he was always greeted with a meery shout by all the men about.

The petty officers' mess was just outside the wardroom door, and was presided over by "Billy" Wilson, who could make a potato scouse

1. Short for "lobscouse," a sailor's stew usually made of meat, vegetables, and hardtack.
2. Not to be confused with the wardroom cook, who, as noted above, was black.

that was very attractive even to the well-fed wardroom boys. If one of us could coax "Billy" into saving out a spoonful of his toothsome scouse for us, we were happy. Some tidbit from the wardroom table went to him in return.

Nearly three weeks were taken up by repairs to our two gun carriages and sundry other matters also received attention. For one thing the visible parts of the ship—all that was above water—received a coat of black paint, which much tidied-up her rusty appearance. Various supplies and stores were taken aboard, the coal bunkers were filled, and on March 23d we hoisted our anchor and were towed out of Station Creek and to an anchorage near the flagship; here we completed preparations for going to sea again.

On March 25th we got underway in the morning, steamed out to beyond the lightship, were taken in tow by the gunboat *Conemaugh* and headed north. About four o'clock in the afternoon, we turned into the mouth of the North Edisto River, about twenty miles south of Charleston, and came to anchor some miles up river. For some days our crew was regularly exercised at battle practice, and on March 26th all the seamen and ordinary seamen were taken ashore and given an afternoon's target practice with rifles.

On the 27th a tugboat came alongside and delivered several inch-thick iron plates, which were to be put down on the deck over the powder magazine and shell room, to re-enforce the deck in that section. Several mechanics came on board to drill the necessary bolt-holes and secure the plates in place.

On the 28th several army transports loaded with soldiers came into the river and anchored. In the afternoon we hoisted our anchor and steamed down river for about a mile, to opposite some thick woods on the north shore, and fired shells into the woods in various directions. Three or four monitors and as many gunboats joined in this exercise, the object of which was to clear the woods of any Confederate soldiers that might be lurking there. After an hour or more of vigorous shelling of the woods, the soldiers were taken ashore in boats and launches, and proceeded to spread themselves over the large island on which they had been landed.

I had an afternoon's "liberty" ashore two days later, and in roaming about the woods found here and there a fire still burning which had been started by the exploding shells from the ships. The tough-fibered Palmetto trees were very slow in burning, the fire seeming to make practically no progress into the trunks. The palm-like foliage of the trees was most interesting to me, and my afternoon ramble through those South Carolina woods was most enjoyable. On the far-edge of the woods I came upon a picket-post of our soldiers, the men on guard duty at different stations being mostly concealed in the underbrush. About half a mile distant across a field a house could be seen, and the soldiers told me that a squad of Confederate soldiers was seen to enter that house about dark the evening before and was supposed to be still lurking there.

On March 29th our usual quiet was disturbed by a large coal schooner drifting down upon us on a strong flood tide, and there was so little wind she couldn't be got under control. Her bowsprit carried away our forward flagstaff, bent down all the rail-rope stanchions on the forward deck on the starboard side, carried away the galley smoke-pipe and the starboard boat davits, and but for our having been able to pay out our anchor chain rapidly, the schooner might even have sunk us. By letting the anchor chain run out rapidly we were able to swing away from the schooner somewhat and permit her to swing past us.

The different stations of the fleet were now and then visited by licensed trading schooners, really sailing "stores", which brought within our reach goods of various kinds, provisions, etc., and the coming of one of these vessels was always welcomed because it gave opportunity to buy needed supplies. One such vessel had followed the army transports into the river, and one of our boat's crews went aboard her to "do some shopping". When the boat returned, three or four of her crew were manifestly drunk. They soon got to fighting and were quickly in a damaged condition. These men, one of whom was boatswain's mate Vincent, were put in double irons in a coal bunker, and an armed boat's crew in command of Mr. Carter was sent to the schooner. A large demijohn (really a carboy) of whiskey was seized and brought back to the *Nahant*, and was locked up in a small locker beneath the wardroom floor.

On April 1st the mechanics completed the putting down of the re-enforcing plates over the powder magazine and shell room, and was also notable for the arrival of the *Keokuk*, a two-turreted iron clad vessel of a radically different type from the monitors. Her turrets were in reality "casemates", and did not revolve; instead, her two XI-inch guns, one mounted in each turret, could be revolved so as to be fired through either of the four portholes in the turret. The iron hull of the

Keokuk was of what is known as the turtle-back type, which greatly exposed her rounded deck and sides to a direct fire from an enemy's guns.[3]

On the 3d and 4th of April we got everything cleared from the deck and stowed below, and the deck was again thoroughly covered with slush. During the afternoon of the 5th we put to sea in tow of the steamer *Locust Point*, headed north, and soon after dropped anchor among the vessels of the blockading fleet off Charleston.

Fort Sumter, which we well knew was our objective, rose sheer from the water at the entrance to the inner harbor and was perhaps three miles distant, while on Morris Island south of the entrance and Sullivan's Island north of it were decidedly formidable-looking forts and batteries. The famous Fort Moultrie, directly across from Fort Sumter, was easily seen by the naked eye among the fortifications on Sullivan's Island, and there looked to be a good prospect of a decidedly stiff fight ahead. I overheard one officer remark to another, as he laid down the glass through which he had been studying the forts and batteries, "This isn't going to be any such picnic as we had at Fort McAllister."

Early on the morning of the 6th of April, the entire fleet of iron-clads, accompanied by sundry tugboats and tenders, got underway and steamed in over the bar. All came to anchor in the outer harbor, about a mile and a half from Fort Sumter. A row of black dots on the water could be seen extending across the entrance to the inner harbor, and looked to be between Sumter and Moultrie. These we recognized were the much-talked-of (and much-dreaded) obstructions to the harbor entrance.[4]

3. The *Keokuk* was an experimental monitor distinguished by its two non-revolving gun towers. Another unique feature of this vessel was that its armor, rather than plate iron, was composed of alternating iron and wood strips. The *Keokuk* was hit ninety times during the attack on Fort Sumter, and was the only monitor sunk by gunfire.

4. In late 1862 the Confederates stretched a rope and log barrier across the main ship channel between Fort Sumter and Fort Moultrie. In 1863 they added a number of mechanical "torpedoes" or mines to this barrier. These explosive devices, about which very little was known, were the "obstructions" referred to by Hunter.

6 | THE ATTACK OF THE IRONCLAD FLEET UPON FORT SUMTER

WHEN WE STEAMED INTO THE OUTER HARBOR OF CHARLESTON ON the morning of April 6th, everyone expected we would be under the guns of Fort Sumter within an hour, and the signal from the flagship to anchor came as a surprise. It had been well understood that we were to make the attack just upon the top of flood tide, so that in case any vessel should become disabled it would drift out of the zone of fire and towards the sea. The conditions seemed to be just right for making the attack at once,—why should we come to anchor and wait? All of that day and night and half the next day we lay there, waiting. The explanation given in the reports is that it was so hazy over the surface of the water the pilots couldn't clearly see certain ranges which they felt that they must see in order to bring the vessels close up to Fort Sumter, as ordered.[1] Fort Sumter had been built upon the outer edge of a shoal, quite close to the channel leading into the inner harbor, and the Admiral's orders to the Captains were to steam well in, so as to bring the guns to bear upon the north-west face of the fort, and concentrate the fire upon the centre embrasure.

There was little for us boys to do. The galley smokepipe being down, there was no fire for cooking and all meals were served cold. Preparations had been made by cooking a supply of meat for the crew,

---

1. Du Pont reported that the delay was "owing to the condition of the tide and an unavoidable accident. . . ." The accident involved the mine sweeping device attached to the bow of the *Weehawken*. Du Pont to Welles, 8 April 1863. ORN, I, 14:3.

and for the wardroom mess a goodly ham and a large piece of corned beef had been cooked and several loaves of bread baked, so there was plenty to eat. After I had found out a way to make coffee on a shovel of red-hot coals in the fireroom, there was no difficulty about our having hot coffee to drink, and that refreshment was served at each meal. The messes of the crew were supplied with hot coffee or tea by taking the mess kettles back to the fireroom and running into them the scalding-hot water from the condenser.

During this long wait I was glad to spend as much time as possible in the open air. The weather was mild and spring-like, and the gentle sea breeze with which we were favored made it a delight to be out in the open. As the main deck was covered with slush most of the leisure time was passed on top of the turret. All of the forenoon of the 7th we waited, and the only incident was a cannon shot which came skipping over the water towards us, fired from Fort Moultrie or one of the batteries near it. Presumably this shot was just a bit of boyish bravado on the part of "our friends, the enemy" on Sullivan's Island.

About mid-forenoon signal was made from the flagship for the vessel to send boats for mail. When our boat returned, two of the letters brought were for me. While I was reading a letter, one of the boys sitting beside me noticed that the stamp on the envelope was quite loose. Removing the stamp he wet it and stuck it upon the edge of the turret just below the top, remarking "There. One big shot is going to strike just where the stamp is." We boys laughed at his assurance, and I remarked that the stamp would certainly be blown away. Taking out my pocket knife, I made three scratches in the shape of a "crowsfoot" in the paint, directly across the top of the plates of the turret, the tip of the crowsfoot being just above the stamp. Later, when we had come out of the fight and we boys were looking over the shot-marks on turret and pilot-house, I looked for my scratch-marks, and we found that one of the heaviest shots that struck us had struck fairly upon the spot where the stamp had been placed, and that everyone of the eleven inch-thick plates had been broken through. We would never have certainly known it, however, but for the scratch-marks I had made with the blade of my knife. Thirty-five years afterwards I visited the old *Nahant*, when she was on duty in New York harbor during the Spanish-American war, and found the scratch-marks in the paint still faintly visible on the bent-in plates where the shot had struck at the top-edge of the turret, and gleefully pointed them out to the officer who was showing me over the ship. To this day it seems to me remarkable that the lad, Dennis Sullivan, should have exactly located the spot where one of the heaviest shots from Fort Sumter was to strike us.

At noon signal was made from the *Ironsides* (the flagship)[2] to get under way, and then another delay caught us. It had been ordered that the *Weehawken* should lead the line of monitors, and some over-wise individual had devised an apparatus for lifting or exploding any torpedoes which might be encountered in the advance. The *Weehawken* was encumbered with this device, which had been well named "a devil." "It was formed of very heavy timbers crossing at right angles, bolted together, and was about fifty feet in length, shaped not unlike a boot-jack, the bows of the vessel propelling within the notch. The after-ends, or jaws, of the raft were secured by chains to the bows of the vessel".[3] There were grapnels to catch the torpedoes suspended beneath this cumbersome raft. When the *Weehawken* was hoisting her anchor, the chain became entangled with these grapnels, and caused over an hour's delay before the chain was cleared and the anchor hoisted up. Not only that, but the encumberance upon her bows made the naturally unwieldy monitor still more unwieldy and difficult to steer, and but for the tide having turned and begun to run flood again, it is doubtful if the *Weehawken* could have steamed up against the current so as to come within range of Fort Sumter. As the *Weehawken* was the appointed leader of the line, a delay to her held back the entire fleet.[4]

The order of battle was that known as "line ahead", or, as a soldier would state it, "single file". The eight monitors were formed into two divisions, with the frigate *Ironsides* (flagship) between the first and second division. In the first division were the *Weehawken*, *Passaic*, *Montauk*, and *Patapsco;* in the second the *Catskill*, *Nantucket*, *Nahant*, and *Keokuk.*

The distance between the vessels was intended to be one hundred yards, but they steered so badly it was quite impossible to keep close to

2. The *New Ironsides*, named in honor of the old sailing frigate *Constitution* which was known as "Old Ironsides," was an armored steam frigate 230 feet long with a displacement of 3,486 tons. Unlike the monitors, it was ship rigged and carried its armament of fourteen 11-inch smoothbores and two Parrott rifles in broadside. This vessel served as Du Pont's flagship from January 1862 when it arrived in Port Royal, until Du Pont was relieved by John A. Dahlgren in July 1863.

3. The quotation is from Daniel Ammen, *The Atlantic Coast*, vol. 2 of *The Navy in the Civil War* (New York, 1883), 92n.

4. See the report of Rodgers to Du Pont, 8 April 1863. ORN, I, 14:11.

distance. The monitors were extremely heavy, unwieldy vessels, steering badly when conditions were at the best. Being in shallow water increased the difficulty of steering, and when steaming ahead very slowly, the difficulty was still further increased; the clumsy vessels were here pretty nearly unmanageable.

When the signal to get underway was made, our crew was called to quarters, and those of us who were stationed on the berth deck, where we could hear little and see nothing, found the long wait very trying to our nerves. We knew that the engine was frequently started and then stopped again, and supposed the starting and stopping were but incidents of getting the vessels into line formation, but why the long, long delay in opening fire we did not know. It was nearly three hours after the call to quarters that we began faintly to hear the boom of the guns of some of the vessels, and it was ten minutes past three o'clock when our two guns were fired in quick succession.

The relief we all felt when at last our guns spoke out was very great, and we gladly hastened to such duties as came to us. Passing on to the door of the magazine the call for cartridges and shells, seeing these brought to and passed through the door to the turret chamber, shaking the inverted cartridge tub over the tub of water, and then returning it to the door of the magazine, didn't call for furious activity on our part, but, it was *something to do*, and a great relief to our strained nerves.

The leading division had come into action about three o'clock, and soon after that the Admiral, finding the *Ironsides* pretty nearly unmanageable in the shallow water and having had to anchor, ordered the signal: "Disregard the movements of the flagship" to be hoisted. This signal at once set free the vessels in the second division and they steamed past the flagship into close action. The *Nahant* was probably the fastest of the single-turreted monitors, and the *Keokuk*, next her in line, was even faster. These two vessels, the last in the line, steamed ahead at full speed and were quickly in the thickest of the fight.

"Four bells" sounding on the gong in the engine room, which ordered the engineer to go ahead at full speed, was distinctly heard by us on the berth deck, and in a few minutes cannon shot began to strike the *Nahant*. At first the hits were few and scattering, but, as we drew nearer to Sumter, they were more frequent. Captain Downes stated that we went up to within five-hundred yards of Sumter, nearer to that fort than any other vessel, and the shots came down upon us in an irregular staccato. There was about twenty-five minutes' time when we were struck on an average about once a minute.[5]

One of the heavy shot struck our turret fairly, about two feet above the deck and just over the heads of the three of us boys who were standing near the turret-chamber door, and so tremendous was the impact, we all three instinctively ducked our heads. The solid shot was smashed and we clearly heard the pieces rattling down upon the deck above our heads.

While we were coming into close action, our guns were kept as busy as the difficulty of loading and firing them permitted. Both guns were fired seven times each, and a little later the XI-inch gun was brought to bear upon one of the forts and fired for the eighth time, making fifteen shots in all fired by the *Nahant*.

Just after we came under the terrific fire which rained down upon us, three heavy shots struck the pilot-house in quick succession. One of these shots struck just at the base of the pilot-house, where a massive iron ring, some four inches deep by a foot wide, rested upon the top of the turret. This ring was put there as a safeguard, to prevent a shot which might strike there from penetrating at the angle formed by the base of the wall of the pilot-house and top of the turret. The metal of this iron ring was bulged outward and upward, and the inch-thick plates of the pilot-house were bulged outward and downward around the deep dent made by the shot. The result was that the turret and pilot-house were tightly welded together; the turret was "jammed" and could not be revolved.

At almost the same instant, a shot struck the pilot-house close beside one of the peepholes which were cut through the walls to give those on duty inside some view of matters outside. The bolts which held the inch-thick plates together were countersunk into the plates on the outside, the nuts being on the inside. Heavy curtains made of two thicknesses of canvas with hair quilted in between hung around the inside of both turret and pilot-house to prevent the heavy nuts on these bolts from flying if the bolts were struck by a shot, but in the pilot-house there had to be holes cut through this curtain where it covered the peepholes. The shot which struck close beside a peephole struck

5. Downes' official report notes that the *Nahant* was "within 500 yards of Fort Sumter, unmanageable, and under the concentrated fire of, I think, 100 guns at short range. . . ." Downes to Du Pont, 13 April 1863. ORN, I, 14:21–22.

The naval assault on Fort Sumter on April 9, 1863: (top) the *New Ironsides*, Du Pont's flagship, flanked by two monitors; (bottom) three monitors with Fort Sumter in the background. (Library of Congress; U.S. Navy)

squarely on one of the bolts, the bolt broke off close by the nut inside, the nut and bolt-end being driven across the inside of the pilot-house with the velocity of a solid shot.

Quartermaster [Edward] Cobb was at the wheel, Pilot [Isaac] Sofield stood a little behind him and was stooping over a bit to observe what could be seen through a peephole on the other side, and Captain Downes was standing a little to one side of the pilot. The flying nut struck Cobb upon the side of his forehead, tearing off a piece of his skull about five inches long by three wide, inflicting a mortal wound. It next struck Pilot Sofield close beside the spinal column at the base of the neck making a deep cut nearly two inches in length and effecting a paralysis of the body because of the shock to the nerves, so that he dropped as though instantly killed. It then glanced upward and struck the top of the pilot-house, then re-bounded downward upon Captain Downes' foot, inflicting a painful bruise which kept the Captain limping about with the aid of a stout cane for several days.[6]

We on the berth deck knew nothing of this tragedy till the turret-chamber door opened and three men came through bearing the body of poor Cobb, and my first sight of a wounded man was when I heard a gasping moan, turned around and looked directly down upon the gaping wound on the side of Cobb's head. Then, for a few seconds, I wished I was back in Boston.

The wounded man was borne to the wardroom table, which was requisitioned for a surgery when we went into battle. It was quickly seen that the case was hopeless, the wound was mortal, and the unfortunate quartermaster was tenderly moved to his hammock, which was spread down on the berth deck for him.

Two or three minutes after Cobb had been brought down, the inert body of Pilot Sofield was lowered down from the pilot-house to the turret, then lowered to the chamber below and borne to the wardroom table. I was summoned to make ready the berth in Mr. [Ensign Charles C.] Ricker's stateroom for Pilot Sofield, and overheard Dr. Stedman telling his assistant that if the blow had struck half-an-inch to the right, it would have killed the pilot, as it would have smashed the spinal column. Striking where it did it made only a deep and painful flesh wound, but the shock to the spinal cord had effected a paralysis.

6. Hunter's original manuscript incorrectly represents the pilot's name as Schofield. Stoically, Downes does not mention his own wound in his report.

Another man was quite badly wounded at just about the same moment as those in the pilot-house, a seaman named John McAllister. He was one of a gun's crew and was standing beside his gun in the turret. One of the shots striking the turret broke off a piece of iron which weighed seventy-eight pounds. This piece of iron was thrown violently across the turret, in its course striking and bending the rod which operated the steering gear, and then struck down McAllister, injuring him severely.

The steering gear was put out of business by this accident, and there we were: helpless, drifting slowly up towards the obstructions and under the fire of a hundred heavy guns. It was fully ten minutes before the supplementary steering gear in the turret-chamber could be got into working condition. When it was working, efforts were made to so steer the ship that the guns could be again trained upon Fort Sumter, but these efforts were futile, and the *Nahant* was headed out just as the signal for the fleet to withdraw was hoisted on the flagship. The *Nahant* joined the other vessels and all moved down to the former anchorage.

A detailed account of this battle in *The Atlantic Coast* (one of the books on "The Navy in the Civil War", and written by Captain [Daniel] Ammen who commanded the *Patapsco* at the time) thus reports matters on the *Nahant:*

> The vessel was struck thirty-six times, one man was fatally injured, two others severely and four others slightly, all by flying bolts or other fragments inside the pilot-house and turret. Several of the plates on the side armor were badly broken, and at one place, where two shots had struck near each other, the plating was partly stripped from the wood, the backing broken in, and the edging of deck-plates started up and rolled back in places. On the port quarter and side the plating was deeply indented and started from the side to the stern. The deck had two very damaging shots, one near the propeller well, quite shattering the plates and starting twenty-five bolts; another starting the plates and twenty bolts. The smoke-stack received three shots; one pierced the armor, making a hole fifteen inches long and nine broad, displacing the grating inside, and breaking seven bolts. The turret received nine shots; fifty-six bolts were perceptibly broken, the nuts stripped from the inside, and the bolts themselves protruded almost their length; some of them, in fact, having been actually forced out were found lying on the deck; doubtless many others were broken that had not been

detected, as some bolts seemingly sound were afterward found loosened. One shot struck the upper part of the turret, breaking through every plate, parting some of them in two, three and four places. The pilot-house bore marks of six shots, three of XI-inch diameter; twenty-one bolts were broken and others started, and the plates were much started; in the opinion of the commanding officer a few more shots would have demolished it. One of the missles at the base broke through every plate, and evidently nearly penetrated.

During the action the *Nahant* fired seven XV-inch and eight XI-inch projectiles. It was not until 5 P.M. of the next day that the turret was sufficiently cleared to be turned, although a corps of skillful workmen under able supervision were engaged at it.[7]

The shot mentioned in this account as breaking through every plate at the top-edge of the turret is manifestly the one which struck the stamp taken from my letter by Dennis Sullivan, and the shot which broke through every plate at the base of the pilot-house was the one which also struck on the base-ring there and effectually "jammed" the turret, putting the *Nahant* out of business. Captain Ammen is in error, however, in stating that three of the shots which struck the pilot-house were "of XI-inch diameter". Major Johnson of the Confederate army, at the time a captain of engineers and stationed in Fort Sumter, in his authoritative book, *The Defence of Charleston Harbor,* distinctly states that there were no guns larger than X-inch mounted upon the fortifications at this time.[8]

Of the *Keokuk,* the vessel next in line to the *Nahant* and which joined with her in the quick dash into the thick of the fight, Captain Ammen's book says:

> The commanding officer of the *Keokuk* states that at 3.20, the flag-ship having made signal to disregard her motions, we found it necessary to run ahead of the *Nahant* to avoid getting foul of her in a narrow channel and strong tide. In consequence he was forced to take a position slightly in advance of the leading vessel of the line, which brought the *Keokuk* under a concentrated fire between Sumter and Moultrie, about five-hundred and fifty yards from the latter. This position was maintained about thirty minutes, during which time the vessel was struck ninety

7. Ammen, 98–99.
8. (Major) John Johnson, *The Defense of Charleston Harbor* (New York, 1889, 1970), 38.

times. Nineteen shots pierced her at and just below the water-line. The turrets (casemates) were pierced in many places and one of the forward shutters shot away; in short, the vessel was completely riddled.

Finding it impossible to keep her afloat many minutes more under such an extraordinary fire, at 4.40 she was reluctantly withdrawn from action. The gun-carriage of the forward turret was disabled, and so many men of the crew of the after gun wounded as to disable that gun. She was anchored out of range of the fire of the enemy and kept afloat during the night, as the water was smooth. At daylight the breeze sprang up, the leakage increased, and it was apparent the vessel must go down. Signal was made, assistance arrived, and an endeavor was made to get the head of the vessel around to-tow her into shoaler water, but in that effort she filled rapidly and at 7.20 A.M. of the 8th sunk, her smokestack alone remaining partly above water. The wounded had been put aboard of a tug a few minutes before the vessel sunk. The casualties were 16 seriously, and as many more slightly wounded.[9]

It should be stated that the crew of the *Keokuk* was taken off by the tugboat which endeavored to swing her head around, hence no lives were lost in that disaster. The tops of the turrets of that vessel were under water at high tide, but at low water fully half the height of the turrets was out of water, and my diary distinctly states that on April 11th the *Weehawken* fired seven shots at the exposed turrets of the *Keokuk* in an attempt to so damage them as to prevent the Confederates getting out of the guns.

As a matter of fact the Confederates did salvage those two XI-inch guns, and had them mounted on the defences of Charleston harbor when a second attack was made upon them the following July. The method of salvaging those guns is told in Major Johnson's book, which also has the following to say about the doings of the *Nahant* in the attack described above:

Commander John Downes took the *Nahant* into the hottest fire of the forts, but while he could fire only fifteen times his alert adversaries jammed his turret with three blows from heavy shot, put his steering-gear out of order, and caused his vessel to drift, unmanageable for a while, nearer to the forts than any of her colleagues, with the risk of being carried by the flood-tide,

9. Ammen, 99.

then setting in from the bar, upon certain destruction. By strenuous exertion a new arrangement was made for steering, and the ship was saved, but the guns could not be brought to bear, and she had to withdraw from action to repair damages.[10]

When we had anchored in the outer harbor after withdrawing from before Fort Sumter, a feeling of disappointment and chagrin at our failure settled down upon us. We had failed, and failed disastrously, where we had expected at least a fair measure of success. Perhaps we had been too confident of success, but after the success of the *Monitor* in resisting the shots of the *Merrimack* and of the *Montauk* in resisting the shots of Fort McAllister, we had believed that such an ironclad fleet as moved up to attack Fort Sumter was well nigh invulnerable.

And the monitors were vulnerable—there was no doubt about that after our experience with Fort Sumter on April 7, 1863. Admiral Du Pont summoned the captains of the monitors to the flagship that evening for reports and a consultation, and was greatly disappointed to learn that five out of the eight monitors were wholly or partly disabled. When the signal to withdraw from action was hoisted, the Admiral fully expected to renew the attack the next morning. After the several captains had given him verbal reports of the injuries to their vessels, he decided at once not to renew the attack, as in his judgment "it would have converted a failure into a disaster."[11]

Captain Ammen, in *The Atlantic Coast*, writes:

> The result of the attack was mortifying to all of the officers and men engaged in it. Had any loss of life been regarded as likely to render another attempt successful, there would have been few indeed who would not have desired it. The opinion before the attack was general, and was fully shared by the writer, that whatever might be the loss in men and vessels, blown up by torpedoes or otherwise destroyed, (and such losses were supposed probable), at all events Fort Sumter would be reduced to a pile of ruins before the sun went down. The damage to the forts by the very small number of projectiles fired by the vessels, although not known at the time to the assailants, was so considerable as to cause the enemy to fill nearly all of the casemates with sand, and this work was begun and carried on vigorously the very night after the bombardment.

10. Johnson, 53.
11. Quoted in Johnson, 55. For the original see Du Pont to Welles, 15 April 1863. ORN, I, 14:7.

The damage inflicted on the vessels shows that they were incapable of enduring heavy blows sufficiently long to effect the destruction of Sumter, as they were situated, or as it was supposed possible to place them. There was considerable swell even between the forts at the time of the attack, and the flood tide ran strong and irregular, which added to the embarrasment. Afloat, as elsewhere, Leeks have to be eaten sometimes, whether liked or not, as an old proverb has it.[12]

Mention was made of the device which was attached to the bows of the *Weehawken* to "remove or explode torpedoes". Captain Rodgers, of that vessel, in his report of the action states:

We approached very close to the obstructions extending from Fort Sumter to Fort Moultrie—as near, indeed, as I could get without running upon them. They were marked by rows of casks very near together. To the eye they appeared almost to touch one another, and there was more than one line of them.

The appearance was so formidable that, upon deliberate judgment, I thought it right not to entangle the vessel in obstructions which I did not think we could have passed through and in which we should have been caught. Beyond these, piles were seen between Castle Pinckney and the middle ground.

A torpedo exploded under us or very near us. It lifted the vessel a little, but I am unable to perceive that it has done us any damage.[13]

That it had done no damage is evident from the fact that there was *no explosion* of a torpedo under or very near the *Weehawken*, as is proven by the following from Johnson's *Defence of Charleston Harbor.*

Then, with regard to the obstructions seen by some of the more advanced monitors. More than one naval officer reported these as appearing to be very near or "close aboard." But they were certainly known by the Confederates to be upward of three or four hundred yards farther within the mouth of the harbor than any point reached by the Weehawken, the Nahant or the Keokuk. They have been commonly mentioned as being on a line between Fort Sumter and Fort Moultire. This is a mistake: they were originally placed between Sumter and Battery Bee on

12. Ammen, 102–3.
13. John Rodgers to Du Pont, 8 April 1863. ORN, I, 14:12.

Sullivan's Island, but had dragged their anchors a little below the line of Battery Bee. They consisted of parts of a broken boom of heavy logs and of a few sections of rope-netting; but there were positively no torpedoes among them or forward of them on that day; and there was, moreover, an opening, three hundred yards wide between them and Fort Sumter, entirely clear of all obstructions.[14]

In this connection mention should be made of a large "Boiler Torpedo" (more properly speaking a mine) which contained three thousand pounds of powder and was sunk in the channel about one mile off Fort Sumter and half a mile opposite Fort Wagner. This mine was intended to be exploded by an electric spark communicated by a telegraph instrument on Morris Island. The *Ironsides* was known to be exactly over this mine for fifteen or twenty minutes, but the repeated efforts of the telegrapher to explode it failed. The insulation of the wire, or the connection, was defective, and no explosion could be effected.

In a report to the Navy Department dated April 15, Admiral Du Pont wrote:

> I had hoped that the endurance of the ironclads would have enabled them to have borne any weight of fire to which they might have been exposed; but when I found that so large a portion of them was wholly or one-half disabled by less than an hour's engagement before attempting to remove the obstructions or testing the power of the torpedoes, I was convinced that persistence in the attack would only result in the loss of the greater portion of the ironclad fleet and in leaving many of them inside the harbor to fall into the hands of the enemy.[15]

Major Johnson's book gives the total number of shots fired in the action by the Confederates at 2,206, with 76 guns engaged. Of these shots, 810 were fired from Sumter and 863 from Moultrie. The vessels of the fleet fired but 139 shots from 23 guns, and they received 439 hits.[16]

Throughout the fleet there was great disappointment at the poor showing made by the *Ironsides* with her sixteen heavy guns as many

14. Johnson, 60.
15. Du Pont to Welles, 15 April 1863. ORN, I, 14:7.
16. Johnson, 58–59.

guns as all the other vessels combined. It was felt that if she could have been brought up near enough to bring her guns to bear upon Sumter on one side and Moultrie on the other, with both broadsides working, great execution would have been done. As a matter of fact, she fired but eight shots, and those at such long range they did but little damage. The armament of the *Ironsides* consisted of fourteen XI-inch guns and two 150-pounder rifled guns, eight guns in each broadside.

Captain Downes had remained at his post in the pilot-house of the *Nahant* until she was safely back at the anchorage, then came limping along the berth deck and through the wardroom to his cabin, where Doctor Stedman took him in charge. Fortunately he had had the good sense to have his boot removed from the injured foot before it was much swollen, but by the time the doctor got it in his hands, it was so badly swollen he could not determine whether any bones were broken, and it was a day later before the swelling was sufficiently reduced to make sure that the severe bruise was the only injury. Had the foot been given complete rest, a rapid recovery would no doubt have followed, but the signal from the flagship for the captains of the monitors to come on board was reported to the captain while the doctor was at work upon the foot. Captain Downes insisted that he wasn't "disabled", limped to his gig, and went on board the flagship to report. Our boats had been taken in charge by one of the attending tugboats when we went into action, and as soon as the monitors were anchored the boats were returned to them again.

All of us were so greatly depressed by our failure, and the evident fact that the monitors were by no means invulnerable there was little disposition to eat supper. Close attention was given to Pilot Sofield, whose nerves were beginning to recover tone. He gradually recovered the use of his limbs, and in a day or two was quite himself again excepting for the deep cut at the base of his neck. In a week or ten days, he was wholly well and back on duty again. But quartermaster Cobb's life ebbed rapidly away. He died a little after midnight, and his body was taken to Port Royal for burial.

A group of machinists were brought on board about seven o'clock that evening, and at once set to work upon the turret and pilot-house where the big shot had jammed them together. They worked industriously all night and the next day, and just before night on the 8th, the obstructing metal had been cut away so that the turret could be turned a little. Then it was found that the machinery which turned it worked quite badly. It was fully three weeks before the machinery was got to working right and the *Nahant* was a fighting ship once more.

With the aid of a glass, large shot holes could be seen in the walls of Fort Sumter, and we found comfort in the thought that we had done some damage with our shells. In fact, after the first heavy depression over our failure, we began to feel that we had got off fairly well, that it might have been very much worse. The sinking of the *Keokuk* was good evidence of what might have happened to any of us, and we were grateful that our ship had escaped a like fate.

For five days we lay at anchor, waiting. It soon became known that the attack was not to be renewed and the crew went to work at cleaning the slush off the deck, getting up the boat davits, and preparing to return to Port Royal. On April 12th we got ready for sea and crossed the bar, were taken in tow by the gunboat *Powhattan* and headed south. On the 15th we arrived at Port Royal, and the next day steamed up into Station Creek again, moored the ship stem and stern and awaited Repairs.

7 ‖ Again Repairing Damages
‖ Restoring the Crew
‖ Blackberrying Pleasures

For three months following the attack upon Fort Sumter, the ironclads in the South Atlantic Squadron did no active service as a fleet. This was chiefly due to conflicting orders from the Navy Department and the President in Washington, but partly due to the fact that more than half the vessels were not in effective fighting condition, and to Admiral Du Pont's conviction that it was a useless risk of ships and men to attack such a strongly fortified position as Charleston without the cooperation of the army with the fleet.[1]

On the evening of the day of our attack upon Sumter, Admiral Du Pont received the following dispatch:

Confidential.　　　Navy Department, April 2, 1863.

Sir——The exigencies of the public service are so pressing in the Gulf that the Department directs you to send all the ironclads that are

---

1. Du Pont had been dubious all along about pitting the monitors against masonry fortifications like Sumter. He believed the failure of the assault on 7 April was due to the inability of the monitors to stand up to such a pounding, and he wanted the details of the assault made public in order to remove blame from himself. Lincoln and Welles, however, did not want to release the details of the assault as it would undermine the public's faith in the monitors which northern public opinion had come to regard as the decisive weapon of the naval war. Du Pont therefore asked to be relieved and he was replaced on 6 July by Rear Admiral John A. Dahlgren. In effect, Du Pont became the scapegoat. Du Pont did not receive another command and died in Philadelphia two months after end of the war on 23 June 1865.

in a fit condition to move, after your present attack upon Charleston, directly to New Orleans, reserving to yourself only two.

Very respectfully,

Gideon Welles.[2]

[Nine days later, and before news reached Washington of the Navy's repulse, Welles sent Du Pont another letter.]

It has been suggested to the Department by the President, in view of operations elsewhere and especially by the Army of the Potomac, that you should retain a strong force off Charleston, even should you find it impossible to carry the place.

You will continue to menace the rebels, keeping them in apprehension of a renewed attack, in order that they may be occupied, and not come North or go West to the aid of the rebels with whom our forces will soon be in conflict. Should you be successful, as we trust and believe you will be, it is expected that General Hunter will continue to keep the rebels employed and in constant apprehension, so that they shall not leave the vicinity of Charleston. This detention of ironclads, should it be necessary in consequence of a repulse, can be but for a few days.

I trust your success will be such that the ironclads can be or will have been despatched to the Gulf when this reaches you.

There is intense anxiety in regard to your operations.[3]

Two days later than *the date* of this letter, the Department received the despatch of Admiral Du Pont, telling of the repulse of the attack of the ironclads and that more than half of these vessels were so badly damaged it was necessary that they be sent to Port Royal for repairs, and the President immediately sent him the following message, (presumably by telegraph to Fortress Monroe, then by despatch boat):

Executive Mansion, April 13, 1863.

Hold your position inside the bar near Charleston; or if you have left it return to it, and hold it until further orders. Do not allow the enemy to erect new batteries or defences on Morris Island. If he has begun it drive him out. I do not order you to renew the general attack. That is to depend upon your discretion, or a further order.

2. Welles to Du Pont, 2 April 1863. ORN, I, 13:803.
3. Welles to Du Pont, 11 April 1863. ORN, I, 14:124.

To Admiral Dupont

A. Lincoln.[4]

The President is, of course, the Commander-in-Chief of the Army and Navy of the United States, and, consequently, his word is law. Undoubtedly his order that our position in the outer harbor of Charleston be held was wise, and if that order had been obeyed, the guns of the *Keokuk* would not have been salvaged by the Confederates, nor would Fort Wagner have been strengthened into the hard nut to crack which the combined forces of the army and navy found it to be three months later.

The fact that the Navy Department had ordered that the monitors be sent around to New Orleans soon became known among both officers and men, with effects varying according to the differing temperaments of individuals. Personally, I was pleased at the thought of more extended travel and experience, and that I should see the great Mississippi river, which my geography had spoken of as "The father of waters!"

No sooner were we back in Port Royal than there began to be manifest a lower efficiency among many members of the crew, which was generally attributed to the bad air below when the hatches were all on and battened down. We had endured ten days and nights of close confinement between April 3d and 14th, and the general "tone" of the men was distinctly lower than before we started for Charleston. It is not improbable that the unwelcome prospect of our having to spend the summer months in Gulf waters and up the Mississippi River had something to do with this physical depression, and the repulse we had suffered at Charleston may also have been a contributing cause. Certain it is, however, that there was a manifest "depression" among the crew, and the net result of it was the transfer of several men to other vessels or they went North on prize steamers, and three or four of our officers were sent off on sick leave. We received a draft of a dozen men from the receiving ship *Vermont* and new officers to make good the losses.

The *Nahant* steamed up into Station Creek, Port Royal, on April 14th, and we boys at once resumed our fishing pleasures. Nearly

4. Lincoln to Du Pont, 13 April 1863. Roy P. Basler, ed., *The Collected Works of Abraham Lincoln* (New Brunswick, N.J., 1953), 6:170.

everyday's entry in my diary at this time mentions "fishing", and on April 21st appears the significant entry, "In swimming". Every healthy boy well knows the delight of the "first swim" of the season, and that first swim was followed by another on the 23d, after which date we were over the side and frollicking in the water about every afternoon. We had secured a blanket permit from Mr. Harmony, the "Executive Officer", to go in swimming every week-day afternoon by first giving notice to the officer of the deck at the time. Great pleasure and satisfaction this swimming permit gave us.

When Barney Doyle, George Patterson, and I waited upon Mr. Harmony and asked permission to try a swim he chanced to be chatting with Doctor Stedman, and they were sitting by the wardroom table. There was a glint of fun in Mr. Harmony's eyes as he asked "Can you all swim?" Then turning to towards me he said: "You're the youngest boy on the ship, Hunter. Can *you* swim?" He leveled at me in a menacing way a lead pencil he was holding in his hand as he asked the question. "Yes, Sir," I promptly replied, "I can swim a mile. I swam a mile one day last summer!"

Turning to Doctor Stedman Mr. Harmony asked: "How often should the boys be allowed to go swimming, Doctor?" Then, without waiting for the doctor's reply, he turned to me again and asked: "How often did you go in swimming up in New Hampshire. How many times did you go in swimming in one day?" Three or four officers had drawn near, evidently amused at the way Mr. Harmony was quizzing us. When I told him that I went in swimming seven times in one afternoon last summer, audible chuckles were heard.

"How is that, doctor?" asked Mr. Harmony. "Once a day is enough," said Doctor Stedman. Then Mr. Harmony said: "Tell us about those seven swims in one afternoon, Hunter. The doctor thinks *once* a day is enough." "Yes, Sir," I replied. "But it was a very hot day, and four or five of us boys thought we'd go down to the lake and have a big swim. It's about three miles down to the lake, so we took a swim in Tannery Pond, just below the village; then another swim in Deacon Hunter's millpond, a quarter-mile further down the road; then a third swim in Copp's millpond, half-a-mile further along; then to the lake (Winnepesauke), and had our big swim, which, with two or three races on the sand beach, lasted about an hour. On our way back to the village we did the three swims over again, one each in Copp's millpond, Hunter's millpond and Tannery pond, and that made seven swims in all between dinner and supper."

My story had been enjoyed by the listening officers, as was made evident by their smiles, and they smiled again when Mr. Harmony leveled his pencil at me a second time and said: "That was dissipation, Hunter. Don't do it again." "Thank you sir," I replied. "We'll go in swimming only once a day, sir." And we kept my promise. We would go to the officer of the deck and report that we were going in swimming by permission of Mr. Harmony, then betake ourselves aft, strip off our clothes, and plunge over the side.

With the deck but fifteen to eighteen inches above the water, there was no danger whatever if one was a good swimmer. True, there was no railing for us to take hold of when we wanted to come out, but a few feet of rope, with one end made fast to a stanchion and the other end in the water, gave opportunity to draw oneself up till the stanchion could be reached. Then it was easy to climb to the deck.

Mechanics from the machine shop came on board daily and were busily at work upon turret and pilot-house. The top of the pilot-house was hoisted off, and a lining made of boiler-iron plates riveted together was lowered down into it. This "lining" was about an inch smaller all around than the inside diameter of the pilot-house, and would effectually stop all flying nuts and bolt-ends.

On April 17th we received sets of "sectional" rammer and sponge handles for the two guns. These sectional handles were to take the place of the clumsy long handles previously used, and were supposed to be a substantial improvement upon the long handles in that the guns could be sponged out and re-charged without having to pass the long handles out through the portholes before entering the sponges or rammers into the muzzles of the guns, and as the port-stoppers could remain closed, it wasn't essential that the turret be revolved to bring the portholes away from bearing upon the target.

As a matter of fact, however, there was practically no saving of time in re-charging the guns, unless it was in saving the time consumed in turning the turret a third to half-way around and then back again. The handle sections were locked together by spring catches as each section was passed into the gun, and each section had to be released as it was drawn out, and the time consumed in this locking and unlocking the catches and withdrawing the sponges or rammers in installments was quite as great as with the long handles.

There was daily exercising of the crew at the guns, even if the turret couldn't be revolved, and on April 23d, the repairs being pretty nearly completed, we steamed out of Station Creek and anchored near the flagship. We got under way early the next morning, again steamed north, and about five o'clock in the afternoon again dropped anchor in the North Edisto river.

The mechanics continued their work upon the turret machinery and on April 28th we were able to turn the turret again. It could be turned, but the machinery did not work quite adequately, and it was not until four or five days later that it worked fairly well and we could feel that the ship was again in fighting condition.

The news of our failure at Charleston had been a great disappointment to the people of the North, and the question as to the monitors being able to resist heavy shot was much discussed in the papers, in Congress, etc. One result of the discussion in Congress was the ordering of the *Passaic* to the Washington navy yard, to the end that Congressmen and officials of the Navy Department have opportunity to study the effect of heavy shot upon her armor.

The departure of the *Passaic* for Washington brought a substantial pleasure to the officers and wardroom boys of the *Nahant*, through the presenting of a little boat called a "Dinghy" to our officers. This little boat was the private property of the officers of the *Passaic*. As they did not care to take the little boat with them, they presented it to our wardroom officers, "with the compliments of the wardroom officers of the *Passaic*," when their ship was about to start for Washington.

This tiny boat was just large enough for three persons, say for an officer with two boys to row the boat, and it at once became very popular with both officers and boys. As I was a fairly good oarsman, many pleasure trips came to me by way of this dinghy. The fact that one or another of the boys was frequently undergoing punishment in a coal bunker, while I was always free of that handicap, doubtless aided to my being almost daily on the water in the dinghy.

A serious difficulty with the monitors now became manifest in their dragging their anchors in the strong tides of the North Edisto. The anchors with which the monitors were equipped were not heavy enough to hold such clumsy, unwieldy vessels, and then, too, the marine growth upon our hulls had developed rapidly in the warm water of the South Atlantic. Certain it was that we began to drag our anchor during the strongest of the flow of both the flood and ebb tide, and considerable work was now done in an effort to rid our hull of the barnacles growing there.

A scraping apparatus was drawn back and forth, from one side to the other, under the hull, the scraper being gradually worked backward from bow to stern. This scraping of the hull gave some relief, but it was found necessary to work the engine at slow speed for an hour or two when the tide was running strongest, to keep from dragging our anchor and drifting afoul another vessel.

On May 11th we were treated to a sensation. A deserter from the Confederates came floating down river on the ebb tide and was taken aboard by one of the vessels of the fleet. On being taken to the Admiral he imparted the information that a small force, equipped with spar-torpedoes and rowboats, was concealed in the woods two or three miles up-river, and that it was the plan to make an attack upon the monitors on a favorable night and at the beginning of the ebb tide. In consequence of this information two of the monitors steamed up river and engaged in the pastime of shelling the woods for a couple of hours, and all the monitors were fitted with fenders made of small spars and a spare hawser, to prevent a boat getting sufficiently near to the side of a vessel to use a spar-torpedo effectively.[5]

Armed sentries stood guard about the deck at night, and an armed boat's crew from each one of the ships in turn, the boat in command of an officer, went up-river for a distance of about a mile each night, to give us warning by burning a signal light in case an attack was threatened. The extra duty and wakefulness which came upon both officers and men in consequence of this alarm was the cause of much grumbling, and there gradually grew up strong doubts of the truth of the deserter's story, but that the danger was very real is shown by a few paragraphs in Johnson's *Defence of Charleston Harbor.*

Experiments with spar-torpedoes attached to rowboats which had been encouragingly successful had been made by the Confederates in Charleston, and a fleet of fifteen of such boats had been made ready just inside Cumming's Point, which is the northernmost tip of Morris Island and just south of Fort Sumter. It was intended to make an attack upon the ironclad fleet including the *Ironsides,* which, it will be remembered, had anchored for some days in the outer harbor of Charleston after the repulse of April 7th. The withdrawal of the monitors to Port Royal and the *Ironsides* to the blockading fleet outside the bar frustrated this plan. A month later the monitors were again assembling in the North Edisto, and early in May the Con-

---

5. The torpedo boat force was commanded by Captain William H. Parker, C.S.N., who provides an equally interesting view of this same sequence of events in his memoirs, *Recollections of a Naval Officer* (New York, 1883; Annapolis, 1985), 339.

federates decided to move some of the boats over into the North Edisto and make an attack upon the monitors anchored there. The concluding paragraph of Major Johnson's account of this movement reads:

> It was on May 10th that Captain W. H. Parker, C.S.N., having Lieutenant Glassell for second in command, took through Wappoo Cut into Stono, and down to Edisto, six small torpedo-boats. They were secretly and successfully placed in the best position from which to dash upon the monitors. Everything was in the most favorable train and condition when it was discovered that a deserter had made his way to the enemy's vessels and given them notice of their danger. Nothing remained to be done but to bring the boats back with secrecy to Charleston.[6]

All through May and the first week in June there were many pleasure trips taken in the dinghy. An officer not on duty in the forenoon would ask two of us boys to row him up river a little way, fishing, or in the afternoon an officer off duty would ask to have two boys set him on shore, and tell the boys to go off and find some blackberries while he went to make a call upon some friend in the army encampment. In fact, my first trip ashore with the dinghy was on the first afternoon that we had it, and I was away somewhere in it an average of four or five times a week.

Some entries in my diary read:

> May 16. Went fishing in the dinghy in forenoon.
> 17. Sunday. Divine Service on deck in forenoon; ashore in dinghy in afternoon.
> 18. Ashore in dinghy in afternoon blackberrying, got 2½ quarts.
> 20. Ashore in dinghy in afternoon blackberying, got 3 quarts.
> 23. Ashore in dinghy in afternoon, 3 quarts.
> 24. Sunday. Divine Service on deck in forenoon; in afternoon pulled Pilot Sofield and Mr. [W. S.] Neal (our 3rd Assistant Engineer) pulled the other oar. There was barely room for three in that little boat. (It is safe to state that after we had reached shore that Sunday afternoon I made the boat fast and went off after blackberries, eating my fill of that delicious fruit, which was very abundant that spring on the sea-islands about North Edisto.)

6. Johnson, 74–75.

May 27. Was ashore blackberrying with Mr. Carter and about fifteen men in the 1st cutter; all hands got about four bushels,
May 29. Ashore with Mr. Ricker and a crew in 1st cutter, blackberrying. Walked about three miles, visited two plantation houses which were deserted. Got a lot of flowers and plums, got 3½ bushels of berries.

On each of these two expeditions to plantations, which were some miles up one or another of the estuaries opening into the North Edisto, the men were armed with loaded rifles, and while most of us were picking berries, three men would be standing guard, perhaps a quarter-mile out beyond where we were picking.

On one of these expeditions, two men were seen lurking in the edge of the woods a mile or so distant from where we were, but for the most part the whole country-side was deserted, even by the negroes. The plantations which we visited were of those famed for the valuable "sea-island cotton" grown there, and the blackberries were growing in the former cotton fields.[7]

These berries grew on running vines, the vines growing out of the low ridges on which the cotton plants had formerly grown. We could look along the straight rows of dark-brown earth for perhaps a mile, and those low ridges strikingly suggested the top of a man's head with the hair parted in the middle; the vines, running each way into the shallow depressions between the ridges, were absolutely black with berries. Hundreds and hundreds of bushels of blackberries were going to waste there in May and June, 1863.

On June 10th we were treated to our second sensation by Confederate deserters. On that morning Mr. Carter had asked that Barney Doyle and I go up river him him, fishing. We pulled up river for perhaps half-a-mile, and dropped over our kedge about half way between the shore and a gunboat anchored out in the river. I caught the first fish, which proved to be a small dogfish and it was thrown overboard after its throat had been slit open.

Just as I was ready to drop by hook overboard again I caught sight of a man's head showing just above the sedges growing along the shore;

7. "Sea island cotton," also called long staple cotton, was long, fibrous cotton used in the production of fine linens. It was more prized than the boll cotton but could not be grown inland. Most of the sea island plantations were abandoned by their owners when Du Pont's fleet captured Port Royal Sound.

telling Mr. Carter what I had seen we all three watched the shore for further signs, Mr. Carter being rather inclined to jolly me for "imagining" I had seen a man's head there, and he hinted that I was afraid. I modestly suggested that we were within easy musket-shot of the shore, and that if there were men there who were inclined to shoot at us they would certainly try to hit an officer, rather than Barney or me.

After a few minutes' watching, a head again appeared above the sedges, then a second head appeared, and in a few seconds they dropped down out of sight again. Mr. Carter rapidly reeled up his line, saying: "Pull up the kedge, Hunter. We'll go aboard the gunboat and ask to have a boat sent ashore to investigate."

We pulled out to the gunboat and Mr. Carter went up the ladder and over the side. In a few minutes we heard the boatswain's whistle, then an order passed, then eight or ten men armed with rifles and cutlasses came down the ladder and took their places in a boat moored alongside. Mr. Carter and an officer wearing side arms came down the ladder and stepped into the boat, and Barney and I sat there in the dinghy, watching them as they pulled away towards the shore.

As the boat neared the shore, two of the sailors were holding their rifles at the "ready". Presently we saw the two heads appear, then two men stepped out of the sedges. Four of the sailors, with rifles at the "ready", stepped ashore from the boat, and the officer with his sword drawn joined them. There was some search of the sedges near the riverbank, but the two men seemed to be the only ones about. They stepped into the boat and sat down, the sailors and officer returned to the boat, and it was rowed back to the landing-stage beside which we were waiting.

The two men got out and went up the ladder, followed by the two officers and most of the sailors. One or two of the latter stopped to speak to us and told that the two men were workmen who had escaped from Charleston a few days before. About an hour later Mr. Carter again came down the ladder and took his seat in the dinghy. He looked at me somewhat quizzically for a bit, then said: "Some more deserters," and as it was nearing dinner time we pulled back to the *Nahant*.

The information which was given up by the two men had an immediate influence upon the fortunes of the officers and men of the *Nahant*, and it was to the effect that a powerful ironclad Ram, known by Admiral Du Pont to be in process of building at Savannah, Georgia, was now completed and about to make a dash for the open sea, and then raid the wooden vessels on blackading duty up and down the coast. The Savannah river had been effectually closed five or six months before by the siege and capture of Fort Pulaski near the mouth of that river,[8] and the only way for the ram to escape to sea was through an inlet known as Wilmington River, which opened into Wassaw Sound, from which there was a channel opening out into the ocean some ten or a dozen miles south of the mouth of the Savannah. The *Cimmarone*, one of the light-draft double-ender wooden gunboats designed especially for navigating rivers and shoal waters, was on blockade duty at Wassaw Sound, and shortly after our repulse at Charleston the monitor *Weehawken* had been ordered there, because of the expectation that the Ram would attempt to escape by that channel.

The next day after the coming of the two deserters, the *Nahant* was ordered to join the *Weehawken* on blockade duty at the mouth of Wilmington River. Our deck was at once cleared and we prepared to go to sea, but a violent storm had come on and we waited until the morning of June 13th, then started south in tow of the gunboat *Prometheus.* The storm had passed, but there was still a very heavy sea running and I was wretchedly seasick all day. We croosed the bar and came to anchor in Wassaw Sound about nine o'Clock that evening.

8. Fort Pulaski fell to Union forces on 11 April 1862 after a two-day bombardment.

8 ‖ THE CAPTURE OF THE RAM *ATLANTA*

SOON AFTER DAYBREAK ON THE MORNING OF JUNE 14TH I was on deck, and my first thought as I looked out over the water was: "Where is Wassaw Sound and where is Wilmington River?" That end of Wilmington River is a broad bay and the bay broadens out still more above the point of Tybee Island on the north. It was apparently some three of four miles from the nearest point of Tybee Island to the shore of Great Wassaw Island on the south. It was not easy to see where the river became sound nor where the sound became the ocean. This much was included in my first look-around in the early morning light, but after the tide ebbed there wasn't quite so great breadth of water. The wooden gunboat *Cimmarone* was at anchor some three-fourths ·of a mile to the eastward and the monitor *Weehawken* lay about a half-mile to the west.

A little later, while the officer of the deck was drinking his cup of coffee, I got a few minutes chat with quartermaster Bickford, who was on watch, and borrowed the spyglass for a minute or two to get a better look at the shores. Bickford told me there were extensive mud-flats making out from each of the two islands and that the *Weehawken* was anchored just by the mouth of the river. The gunboat was just outside the bar separating Wassaw Sound from the ocean, and the channel out to the ocean was close to where the gunboat was anchored.

Captain [John] Rogers of the *Weehawken* was the ranking officer of the three vessels present, hence was the commanding officer of the little fleet. Captain Downes went aboard the *Weehawken* directly after

73

breakfast to consult with Captain Rodgers as to what would be the plan of action if the Ram came down the river. After Captain Downes returned in the afternoon, we hoisted our anchor and steamed over to a position just below the *Weehawken*.

The crew was exercised at quarters both forenoon and afternoon, and just after dusk the 1st cutter, in command of Mr. Carter and with the boat's crew well armed, went off up-river for a mile or more on picket duty, to give warning by burning a Costan's signal-light[1] if a vessel was discovered trying to run out to sea; the boat returned just after daybreak.

During the next day a large, black steamer came down river to within two or three miles of us. It could be seen with a spyglass that she was not a war ship, and she disappeared again without coming down towards the mouth of the river. We supposed that she was reconnoitering. That night the picket boat was sent up river from the *Weehawken*.

During the forenoon of the 16th, the large, black steamer came down in sight again and we cleared for action, but she returned up river after a little while. The crew was drilled at small-arms and at target practice, and that evening one of our boats was sent up river on picket with Pilot Sofield in command.

It was talked among the officers in the wardroom that if the Ram came down river, she would most probably make a dash for the open sea, and it would be our play to stop her if we could. The *Weehawken* would be nearest to her and would have the first chance. If she got out past the *Weehawken*, we would head her off from getting to sea if possible. As the Ram was reported to be much faster than the monitors, and to draw more water, our best chance seemed to be to get into the channel and crowd the Ram into shoaler water if she attempted to run past. Also we would give her as many solid shot as possible and at as close range as possible.

Our anchor chain was uncoupled at a coupling-link a few feet inside the capstan, and a small buoy with a stout rope attached lay on the deck close by the bow, the other end of the forty or fifty feet of rope being secured to the anchor chain just outside the bow. One of the men was standing sentry near the bow, and in case of an alarm he was to toss the buoy overboard, then release the capstan and let the few

---

1. Costan's signal light was a slow-burning pyrotechnic flare invented by B. F. Costan in 1840. Its principal feature was that it could change colors to indicate specific messages.

feet of chain run out, and the ship would be free from her anchor at once. The boats were floating astern, attached to a line, and would follow us into action.

The galley smokestack was taken down each evening and everything cleared from the deck, excepting that the berthdeck and fireroom hatches were left off but suspended in such a position they could be dropped into place in a few seconds. About three-fourths' head of steam was kept up in the boilers, both guns were loaded with solid shot, and we were all ready for instant action should the alarm be sounded.

Early the next morning I awoke to consciousness with the thought: "Today is the 17th of June and they will be celebrating 'Bunker Hill Day' in Charlestown; wish I could be there!" I lay quietly in my hammock for a few minutes, then noted a faint gray light just showing down the berthdeck hatchway and thought: "Its almost morning, guess I'll get up."

Slipping quietly out of my hammock so as not to disturb the men sleeping all about, I dressed, then lashed up the hammock and had unhooked one end of it when I heard rapidly running feet on the deck above, and the quartermaster came running-tumbling down the ladder. He seized the boatswain's mate by the arm and exclaimed: "Call all hands, quick, sound to quarters. She's coming right down upon us!"

In a flash I had tossed my hammock into the hammock-room door and hurried on deck. I was around the turret and on my way aft before the call to quarters sounded through the ship. The tide was still running flood, so it was necessary that I get abaft the smokestack to get an unobstructed view up river. Just as I passed the smokestack our picket boat came along at top speed, every man pulling his oar for all he was worth, and Pilot Sofield's face had a tense and anxious look upon it.

About a mile distant was the Ram coming down towards us at a fast clip, as was evident from "the bone in her teeth" (the jet of foam turned up by her bow), and I could distinctly see a small spar standing almost straight up from a light framework on her bow, with a black object about the size of a nail-keg on top of it. This last I "sensed" at once was a spar-torpedo.

As I stood on the exteme point of the stern, with one arm crooked around the flagstaff for safety, I saw the spar on the bow of the Ram swing forward and down and drop into the water with a splash, and the black muzzle of a gun appeared out of the bow porthole; in two or three seconds there was a flash from the gun and a shot struck the water perhaps a third of the distance between the Ram and us. Then I saw the big-looking black shot rising and coming straight towards where I was standing. I could see that cannon shot as plainly as the catcher sees the balls which a pitcher throws to him.

The shot struck the water some forty to fifty feet away, dashing up a great quantity of water which came down on the afterend of the *Nahant* in a torrent and wet me to the skin, and then I saw the shot go past, tumbling end over end upon the water, and making such a roaring as I imagine might be made by a small tornado. That "roar" in my ears, added to the ducking I had received, brought me to realize that I was where I had no business to be. The throbbing of the propeller under the overhang told that the engine was working, and I started forward to get below, shouting out in glee: "It's Bunker Hill Day, and Great-Grandfather Folsom fought at Bunker Hill! We'll whip 'em."

Three of the men had been dropping the fireroom hatch into place and were disappearing into the turret through the XI-inch gun-port as I hurried past. Seeing that the berthdeck hatch was just about to be dropped into place, I made a rush for the open hatchway and jumped down, catching my fingers on the edge of the hatchway to break my descent.

Mr. Ricker was the officer in charge of the berthdeck when we went to quarters and he was standing just beneath the hatchway. Grasping my arm he demanded: "Where have *you* been! Why,—You're wet. Have you been overboard?" Telling him I was wet by water dashed up by a shot fired at us from the Ram, I escaped further attention through his being busy seeing the hatch secured in place, and I joined the boys at our station.

There were but three of us boys by the turret-chamber door at first as George Patterson was undergoing punishment in one of the coal bunkers. He was soon released, however, as it was a regulation that no one should be shut up in irons when a ship went into action so that all might have equal opportunity for escape in case of accident.

The boys were greatly interested in the story of what I had seen, and this story I had ample time to tell because for half an hour or more we were all quiet below. The engine was throbbing and we could hear the rudder chains moving now and then. Five or six decidedly audible "booms" from outside came to our anxious ears, so we knew the *Weehawken* was busy and thought it probable the Ram was also busy, but our guns were silent.

Once, indeed, we heard the call "Are you all ready?" and the answer: "All ready, Sir." and then the command: "Fire!" But no gun responded. Instead we heard some words of explanation, and afterwards learned that the gun was pointing directly at the side of the armored part of our smokestack, a fact which Mr. Harmony could not know because he was sighting through the peephole three or four feet to the right of the gun. If the gun had been discharged we would have shot away one side of the lower section of our smokestack. This very accident happened to one of the other monitors a few weeks later.

After we had waited in suspense for a half-hour or more, the order came down from the turret to pass up a dozen cutlasses, revolvers and belts, and for the crew of the 2nd cutter to come on deck. This was very puzzling and we waited for light, which pretty soon came in the order to "pipe down" and lift off the hatches.

We boys were soon on deck, and there lay the Ram a quarter-mile away, the *Weehawken* with her guns trained upon her was quite close and the United States flag flying from the Ram's flagstaff. Two of the Nahant's men with cutlasses in their hands were doing sentry duty, one on the forward deck of the Ram and the other near the flagstaff which stood above the after end of her armored casemate. It was plain that she was our prize.

The action had been brief, and decisive! The Ram had fired two or three shots and all had missed the target. The *Weehawken* had fired five shots, had scored four hits, and two of those shots had settled the fight. Three of the Weehawken's shots had been fired from her XI-inch gun and two from the XV-inch gun. Of the three XI-inch shots one went high and passed over, one struck the edge of the Ram's armor where it bent down and curved under the casement, forming a knuckle, and it broke off some of the iron plating, and the third struck a port-stopper, smashing it and driving the fragments in upon the gun deck.

The first of the two shots from the XV-inch gun, a "cored" shot[2] weighing 420 pounds, struck the inclined side of the armored casemate just about in line with the port-holes and about half way between the forward and 'midship ports. This armored casemate, with sides which inclined at an angle of about fifty degrees, was built of sixteen inches of solid wood and covered with four inches' thickness of iron armor. It

---

2. Cored shot had a hard metal core surrounded by softer iron. Upon impact, the inner core was supposed to be able to penetrate iron armor.

seemed practically certain that a shot striking the armor of so stout a casemate at such an angle would glance off, doing little if any damage, but the XV-inch shot from the *Weehawken,* fired at about 200 yards distance smashed through the casemate, the shock of the impact prostrating about forty men, sixteen of them being badly wounded by the flying splinters.

The gun's crews of the bow and 'midship guns were standing at ease between those two guns and grouped just in line with this shot, in the best possible position to be injured by it. It was the men of those gun's crews that were cut up by the flying splinters.[3] The shot itself did not penetrate; it was smashed in pieces by the impact and the pieces flew over the top of the casemate or slid down the steep incline into the water, but there was a hole smashed clear through the casemate, which, at a little distance, looked to be as large as the head of a flour barrel.

The pilot-house of the Ram was a truncated pyramid, the top-half above and the remainder below the top of the casemate. The four sides of the pyramid were of iron armor and wood backing, similar to the sides of the casemate, and the top which was about two and one-half feet square, was protected by iron bars two inches thick by six inches wide, which were loosely set in slots made for them; there were two-inch spaces between the bars, which sat up edgewise, and the bars were lengthwise of the ship. When the engine of the Ram was stopped as the *Weehawken* was seen to be approaching, her helm was ported very slightly, and she had slowly turned so that her starboard side was presented to the *Weehawken.*

The second XV-inch shot struck the top of the Ram's pilot-house, raking directly across those iron bars and smashing them down upon the heads of the two pilots and helmsman standing just beneath. All three men were badly wounded by the flying pieces of iron, the wheel was temporarily jammed, and just at that moment the Ram touched on the mud bottom!

It is not at all surprising that the Ram had had enough—and surrendered! Such an accumulation of disasters, all coming upon her within a few minutes time was quite sufficient to take the fight out of a far better disciplined crew than most ships could muster. Captain

---

3. The Confederate crew aboard the ram *Atlanta* suffered one dead and sixteen wounded in the brief engagement, though many others were rendered temporarily senseless by the concussion of the large shells striking her armored hull.

Rodgers of the *Weehawken* in commenting upon the action, is said to have remarked: "The first XV-inch shot took away their disposition to fight, and the second their ability to get away!"[4]

And the *Nahant* hadn't got in a single shot! We were much mortified and disappointed at the outcome; we did so much "want to have a hand in the fracus," as one of the officers phrased it at the breakfast table at little later.

And we all felt the fine courtesy of Captain Rodgers of the *Weehawken*, in ordering that an officer and boat's crew from the *Nahant* should board the Ram and receive the surrender. That act stood out so prominently, and was of such delicate courtesy, it quite smothered our grumbling and soothed our disappointment at having had no hand in the fight itself. One of our officers was inclined to scoff at the idea that it was a fine courtesy on the part of Captain Rodgers, and insisted that it was simply good strategy. He maintained that the surrender came so suddenly that Captain Rodgers was taken by surprise, and was inclined to doubt the evidence of the white flag which had been set on the Ram's flagstaff, and that it was "good strategy" to have an officer from the *Nahant* board the Ram while the *Weehawken* kept her shotted guns trained upon her, then if there was anything "foxy" attempted the *Weehawken* could checkmate the move. That certainly is plausible, and, from a purely military standpoint, it is good reasoning. Nevertheless the greater part of our officers and men welcomed the "fine courtesy" suggestion, partly, no doubt, because it was so comforting.

One anecdote connected with the surrender of the Ram is interesting. The preparations for a dash out to sea hadn't included any such act as surrender, consequently no white flag was in the flag-locker. The man who lowered the Confederate flag and bent on and raised a white one was seen to emerge hastily from the Ram's bow port, climb to the top of the casemate and run aft to the flagstaff, lower the large battle-flag from which he tore off a square-yard of the body of the flag, bend it onto the halyards by two corners, and run it up to the peak. This Confederate flag was of a new type, and we were told that this was the first time it had been borne in battle. The body of the flag was white,

---

4. This line is not included in Rodgers's official report to Du Pont dated 17 June. ORN, I, 14:265–66.

The *Weehawken* (left) fires on the grounded *Atlanta* (center) while the *Nahant* (right) looks on in this artist's conception from Harper's Weekly artist W. T. Crane. (U.S. Naval Institute)

The Confederate ram *Atlanta* photographed lying at anchor in the James River after being taken into Federal service.

and it was a small section of this white field that served as a token of surrender.⁵

When the boys came on deck after the hatches were hoisted off, two steamers could be plainly seen, apparently waiting, two or three miles up river, and signal was made by the *Weehawken* for the *Cimmarone* to steam up river to investigate them.

The *Cimmarone* had slipped her anchor chain and sounded her crew to quarters when the alarm was given that the Ram was coming out. A few minutes after she received the order, with her guns run out and crew standing at their stations, she steamed past us at top speed, but the suspicious-looking steamers hurried away and disappeared around a bend in the river as soon as their officers saw the gunboat coming up after them.

We learned a little later in the day that those two steamers were loaded with enthusiastic and confident friends of the officers and crew of the Ram, who had accompanied her down from Savannah to witness the triumph of their friends and relatives and discomfiture of the Yankees. How great must have been their disappointment at the result!

That it was fully believed the Ram would triumph was told to me in confidential chats which I had with two of her younger officers, and was shown in comic pictures which were found drawn on her log-slates. One of the log-slate pictures showed one monitor sinking from the effect of an exploded torpedo, the Ram then in the act of turning to attend to the other monitor upon which the flag was being hastily lowered in token of surrender, members of the crews of both monitors being pictured as diving over their sides in panic.

Soon after the *Cimmarone* had started up-river, another steamer hove in sight to the northward, coming down towards us at high speed. When she was near enough to be made out through a glass, it was seen that she was flying the United States flag, and in a short time she reported herself as the U.S. Army steamer *Island City* sent down from Fort Pulaski to ascertain the meaning of the heavy guns which had been plainly heard there. The army officers were greatly pleased at the result of the brief fight, the more pleased because the wooden steamers

---

5. Known popularly as the "stainless banner," this particular version of the Confederate flag was often confused with a flag of surrender since the white folds obscured the red and blue jack. For that reason, a red bar was later added to the bottom of the white field.

of the army transport service would have been in great danger if the Ram had succeeded in getting out to sea.

Our galley smokepipe had been put up directly after the Ram had surrendered, and breakfast was ready and served at the usual time. Just as our officers had finished beakfast, a boatload of the officers of the Ram came alongside (about half of them were taken to the *Weehawken*), and they were invited down to the wardroom to breakfast.

We had not been in touch with a supply steamer for two weeks or more and some stores were low. We boys felt that we hadn't a very good breakfast to offer our guests, but one of the Confederate midshipmen, a young chap about my own age with whom I had a considerable chat, told me it was the best breakfast he had eaten in some time, and that the coffee served to them at our mess table was the first "sure-enough coffee" he had tasted in six months. As he was a son of one of Savannah's prominent and wealthy families, it certainly was a tribute to the efficiency of the blockade that his family had been deprived of real coffee for so long a time.

This young Confederate midshipman told me that the building over of the blockade-running steamer *Fingal,* and making her into a man-of-war which was re-named *Atlanta,* had been a pet project of the best people of Savannah for a year or more, that the funds to pay for work and materials had been raised by popular subscription and by giving church fairs, lawn-fetes, etc., and that some families had contributed jewels as well as money to the cause.

His own family had been deeply interested in the work and his father, mother and two sisters, also three or four cousins, were passengers on one of the two steamers which had accompanied the *Atlanta* down river, and which had waited at a safe distance to witness the expected overthrow of the two monitors and capture or destruction of the wooden gunboat stationed there.

The bitter disappointment of those confident men and women can easily be imagined. In a very few minutes the powerful war-ship that they had been so deeply interested in, and which was officered and manned by their relatives and friends, had been defeated and captured by a vessel of less than half her available strength. The officers and crew of the *Atlanta* numbered 142, almost exactly the number of officers and men on both the *Weehawken* and *Nahant.* The *Atlanta* carried four heavy, rifled guns, the same number of guns as the two monitors together, And our guns were all smooth-bores, their round shots having less than half the penetrating power of the bolts fired from the splendid English rifled guns on the *Atlanta.*

One of the books on the Navy in the Civil War, Prof. [James R.] Soley's *The Blockade and the Cruisers,* after narrating the effort made by Confederate ironclads to raise the blockade off Charleston in the winter of 1863, says:

> The next attempt of the Confederates to raise the blockade on the South Atlantic station resulted disastrously to its projectors. This was the brief cruise of the *Atlanta,* formerly the *Fingal,* in Wassaw Sound, in June 1863.
> The *Fingal* was an iron steamer of English origin, which had run the blockade of Savannah in November, 1861. She had been taken by the Confederate Government, re-named the *Atlanta,* and altered and strengthened for service as a man-of-war. In making the alterations, she had been cut down so as to leave the deck about two feet above the water when loaded. From this deck rose a casemate, with a flat roof and inclined sides. Within the casemate were four Brooke rifles, two VI ⁴/₁₀-inch in the midship ports, and two VII-inch on pivots at the bow and stern, so contrived that they could be fired either laterally or fore-and-aft. The armor protecting this powerful battery was four inches thick, made of English railroad iron, rolled into two-inch plates. The deck was of enormous strength, and its edges projected six feet from the side of the vessel, the projection being filled in and protected with a heavy covering of wood and iron. The *Atlanta's* bow ended in a ram, over which projected a torpedo spar. She was in every way one of the most powerful vessels that the Confederates had got afloat; and great things were expected of her.[6]

And why hadn't the officers of the *Atlanta* made use of their guns, and their ram, and their spar-torpedo? These questions were much discussed by the officers of the *Nahant* as they sat at mess or gathered about the wardroom table in the evenings just following the action; those discussions I listened to with intense interest.

The first question was: "Why did the *Atlanta* stop to fight?" Obviously her best play was to escape to sea and inflict damage upon the wooden vessels on blockading duty up and down the coast, and she

---

6. James Russell Soley, *The Blockade and the Cruisers,* vol. 2 of *The Navy in the Civil War* (New York, 1895), 116.

could almost certainly have escaped if she had made a quick dash past us. She was rated to be a ten-knot ship, and the best speed of the monitors, when they were new and their hulls clean, was about seven knots; now, after six-months' service in southern waters, our hulls were cumbered with much marine growth, and our best speed was not above five or six knots.

It is true the *Atlanta* drew sixteen feet of water while the monitors drew but eleven feet; with her sixteen-feet draft she would need all the depth of water in the channel to get out, and if she edged away to one side to avoid the monitors she would be in great danger of running aground. But when she came down river, both monitors were anchored just to one side the channel and *out in the Sound*. And both monitors had to steam ahead, that is, *out* towards the bar, for several minutes before they could get up sufficient headway to enable them to turn and head up into the channel.

The *Atlanta* was coming down river at a very fast clip when I saw her, and if she had kept straight on as she was going she would have passed out of the river into the Sound before the *Weehawken* had got her head turned up-river. Once in the Sound she should have kept straight on out to sea. The *Weehawken* would doubtless have fired two shots at her as she passed, but going at the speed that she was, it was more than an even chance the shots would miss.

The *Nahant* had no local pilot, hence *had to follow* behind the *Weehawken*. We might (probably would) have got a chance to fire one, or at most, two shots at the *Atlanta* as she passed by, with more than an even chance of missing her at the distance and with our short-bodied smooth-bore guns.

Even if a shot, or two shots, *had* struck the *Atlanta*, she was supposed to be shot-proof, she was supposed to be able to stand punishment, and, at the distance the shots would have to have been fired, and at a rapidly moving vessel of which litle except the casemate showed above the water, the chance of her being seriously injured was extremely remote. Manifestly the officers of the *Atlanta* committed a fatal blunder when they stopped her engine and awaited the approach of the *Weehawken*.

The second question was: "Having stopped as though to fight why didn't she use her guns? Why did she lie there in the river quietly awaiting the approach of the *Weehawken*, and make no use of her superior armament?" She had the best possible opportunity to inflict damage. With her full broadside bearing she could use three guns of heavy calibre and great penetrating power, and during the time the *Weehawken* was slowly approaching and firing five shots at her the *Atlanta* never fired a shot! True, she fired two or three shots (one account says two and another says three), but they were fired at the monitors while they were at least a mile away, and before they had got enough headway to turn and head up-river, but during the twenty to thirty minutes that the *Weehawken* was getting up to close range and then firing five shots at the *Atlanta,* the latter never fired a shot!

That was certainly a great blunder. A vigorous use of her powerful guns, three in a broadside, would have made the task of conquering her decidedly more difficult, and a lucky shot in one of the ports would have so upset the *Weehawken's* gunners as to have given the *Atlanta* the advantage. As it turned out, the two lucky shots were fired by the *Weehawken,* and the *Atlanta* came into our possession, a prize.

The *Atlanta* had touched bottom upon the soft mud-bank making out from Tybee Island at just about the moment the fatal shot struck her pilot-house, but the tide was still a little short of high and she floated off the bank without damage soon after our men had taken possession of her. While the tide was still high, she was guided out of the river into Wassaw Sound under her own steam, and anchored near us.

All of the forenoon the boats of the three United States vessels were busy transporting the officers and men of the *Atlanta* to the *Cimmarone* which steamed away with them in the afternoon to Fort Pulaski, and the prisoners were turned over to the safe keeping of the army authorities at that post. The next day the gunboat *Sebago* arrived early in the morning, and a little later the *Atlanta,* under command of our Mr. Harmony and accompanied by the *Sebago,* steamed away to Port Royal.

The after history of the *Atlanta* is of interest. She was taken north where a prize court condemned her and appraised her value as $300,000. The United States Government bought her at the appraised value and the $300,000 was distributed as prize-money among the officers and men of the three vessels present at the capture. It was the regulation at that time that all vessels of the navy that were within signalling distance participated in the capture of a prize, so the officers and men of the *Cimmarone, Nahant* and *Weehawken* were paid share and share alike, according to their rank, of that prize money. Just about a year later, in June, 1864, I was serving in the Signal Corps,

U.S. Army, and the detachment to which I belonged was encamped on the high bluff just below Natchez, Mississippi, when I received a U.S. Treasury warrant for $176.16 as my share (the share of a 1st Class Boy), of that $300,000 prize money.

The *Atlanta* was fitted up for services in the United States Navy and was on duty with the fleet opeating in the James River till the close of the war. Soon after the war she was sold to the government of Japan, was prepared for and started on the long voyage around Cape Horn, and in due time went into the harbor of Rio de Janerio for coal and supplies. After receiving those she steamed away towards the Staits of Magellan, and was never heard from afterwards.

9 | PLEASURES AT PORT ROYAL

GETTING READY FOR THE NEXT MOVE

A VISIT TO THE RAM *ATLANTA*

ALTHOUGH WE HAD ACCOMPLISHED THE PURPOSE FOR WHICH WE had been sent to Wassaw Sound, the officers and men of the *Weehawken* and *Nahant* did not relax their viligance, and every precaution was taken to guard against a surprise-attack, which was now what we had most to fear. An armed boat's crew from one ship or the other was sent up-river each evening, and armed sentries stood at four different stations on our deck from dark to daylight.

Nothing disturbed us on the night of the 18th, but the next day two or three men thought to be Confederate soldiers were seen lurking in the edge of the woods on Great Wassaw Island which forms the southern shore of Wilmington River. A boatload of armed men was sent ashore to investigate, but it wasn't wise for a few men without supports near at hand to go into the woods for any distance, and nothing hostile was discovered.

Later in the day two armed boats' crews, one of them from the *Cimmarone,* explored the shore of the island for three or four miles up-river and discovered a small schooner concealed in an inlet which made into the island for some distance. The schooner was boarded and taken possession of, and before night had been towed down to near our anchorage by the two boats. Doubtless this small schooner was one of the numerous small vessels that were dashing out from the southern harbors on very dark or stormy nights, taking out a few bales of cotton and bringing in much needed medicines and supplies. As these sloops and schooners drew but a few feet of water, they could slip out and in at unguarded channels along the coast.

With our own crew reduced in numbers by the working party sent away on the *Atlanta*, the extra work coming upon them was wearing upon the men, and the sending of an armed boat's crew on picket every third night was a hard task. Part of the men could get some sleep while the remainder were watching, but sitting or half-lying cramped up in a row boat isn't very restful, and the regular drills and duties were omitted or lightened as much as possible. Some drill and target practice with small arms was indulged in, and each afternoon about half the men went ashore with the seine and had a fine frolic fishing and swimming. Good hauls of fish were brought aboard, and one afternoon they came near having the seine destroyed through having caught a four or five foot shark and he tangled himself up in it. One of the sentries posted on shore saw the commotion, ran down into the water, and succeeded in impaling the shark with his bayonet.

On another afternoon the fishing party found a solid shot which had been fired at the monitors by the ram, and which had gone so nearly ashore it was exposed to view when the tide was well out. The men succeeded in getting this heavy shot into the boat and brought it on board. It was sent to Admiral Du Pont when we returned to Port Royal, and by him was sent to the Navy Department in Washington, where it was placed among the curios and attracted considerable attention. It is certain that this shot was *not* the first shot fired at us, which I had seen fired and which had given me a ducking—from the position of the ram at that time and our position out in the Sound, that first shot must have passed out towards the bar.

On the evening of June 20, our boat's crew went up-river on picket, and just as they were about to drop over the kedge to keep the boat from drifting, two or three small boats were discovered lurking near and what seemed to be a small steamer a little distance behind them. A Costan signal-light was set off to give the alarm, and our crew was called to quarters. The picket boat came racing back to the ship and we waited for developments. After waiting and watching for about an hour without any suspicious sights or sounds, the crew was piped down and the picket boat went cautiously up-river again.

It was surmised that it was the hope to surprise and capture the picket boat before an alarm could be given, then make a surprise-attack upon the two monitors with spar-torpedoes, and that the party retreated up-river after they had been discovered and the alarm given. It certainly would be no more than natural that the friends of the crew of the *Atlanta* should desire revenge, and we were wise to take every precaution against a surprise-attack. After the warning we had received in the North Edisto some weeks before, of an intended attack upon the monitors there by row boats equipped with spar-torpedoes, it was felt that we must maintain constant watchfulness against a night attack.

The day following this night alarm was Sunday. There was general muster and inspection followed by Divine Services in the forenoon, and the afternoon was wholly given over to resting. The next day a sailboat was seen two or three miles up-river and an armed boat's crew was sent up in pursuit, but the breeze freshened and no boat propelled by oars could overhaul a sailboat which had a good and favorable wind, the boat drew steadily away and disappeared towards the Savannah river. That afternoon the *Weehawken* sailed for Port Royal.

On the 25th of June the steamer *Haze* came in with mail for us which included orders for the *Nahant* to return to Port Royal. Preparations for sea were soon made and about noon we passed the outer buoy off Wassaw bar. At 7:30 that evening we dropped anchor near the flagship in Port Royal harbor and a little later Mr. Harmony returned aboard.

For almost two weeks we remained at Port Royal, and those days were the most enjoyable of my year's service in the navy. The *Nahant* was towed up to or near the machine shop and anchored, and a force of mechanics was constantly at work upon the machinery which revolved the turret—which did not work *right*. The chief difficulty was to stop the turret at just the right point to bring the guns to bear upon the target. The guns being mounted upon carriages which moved forward and back upon stationary steel beams, it was essential that the turret be stopped at exactly the right point or they did not aim at the target. If the turret turned an eighth of an inch too far, the shot would go wide of the target, hence to bring the guns to bear exactly right, it would be necessary to reverse the machinery and start the turret back again, then it would probably go too far the other way and another start forward had to be made. It was sometimes necessary to turn the turret back three or four feet, then reverse and start it forward again and try to stop it at exactly the right point. Sometimes, indeed, it was found best to turn it completely in order to bring the guns to bear exactly upon the target. A determined effort was made during this stay at Port Royal to so adjust the revolving mechanism of the turret as to make it dependable—or at least as dependable as the rather clumsy steam machinery of 1862 could be made.

During these Port Royal days we boys had much liberty, especially in the afternoons. Taking the dinghy we went ashore at Bay Point, which is the northern side of the entrance to Port Royal harbor, and there we had delightful swims in the water and frolics on the sandy shore. Sometimes another boy and I were called upon to row one of the officers to Hilton Head which was the army supply station and where there were many stores. One boy would remain with the boat while the other went ashore for an hour, then the first boy would come back and stay with the boat while the other went ashore. During these visits to Hilton Head, I became fairly well acquainted with the small city which had grown up there, and made some acquaintances among the soldiers on duty at that post.

About Bay Point, however, was a scene of desolation. The earthwork there had been pretty well demolished in the bombardment by Admiral Du Pont's fleet, and as the point itself had no value for our troops, it had not been occupied. A single store, kept by a couple of New Yorkers, stood in a small grove of rather stunted trees a quarter-mile back from the shore and there I was able to buy a bar of fresh-water soap of which I felt the need.

We could buy salt-water soap of the purser's steward aboard ship, but as I was able to get a bucket of hot fresh water from the condenser in the engine room at any time, I longed for fresh-water soap. I felt decidedly cleaner after having made that purchase. And in making that purchase I first made the acquaintance of the bank-note detector of those days. Being short of funds, I had mentioned the fact in a letter home, and my father had promptly sent me a two-dollar bill of the local bank in New Hampshire. But that bill of the Belknap County Bank seemed to be of about as much value in South Carolina as a counterfeit bill would be. When I expressed a wish that I could buy a bar of soap, the storekeeper asked if I had any money and I told him I had a two-dollar bill on a New Hampshire bank. "Let me see it," he said. I passed it over to him and he opened the "Detector" and soon told me the bill was perfectly good and that I could buy anything I wanted with it. I secured the coveted soap, some handkerchiefs, and two or three other trifles, then stood treat on sweets and peanuts for the party. I promptly vetoed the suggested treat of whiskey, which one of the boys expressed a desire to try!

On occasion of one of our afternoon visits at Bay Point, we walked back to the little naval cemetary and looked up the grave of poor Cobb, who had been killed in our attack upon Fort Sumter in April. I had been sitting in the naval recruiting office in Boston when Cobb and his chum, both genuine "old sea dogs" and man-o-'war's-men, had come in to ship for the *Nahant,* and the kindly interest of the aged Commodore in them, and his admonitions that they do no more drinking that day, I still vividly remember: "You've had enough for today, boys. Remember now, don't drink any more today!" he had said to them. "Aye, aye, Sir!" they both responded with their knuckles going up to the forehead in salute, and the aged Commodore gazed fondly after them as they passed out of his office. Cobb was from Salem, Massachusetts. He was a small man, rather gruff in manner, but he had always been kind to me, and I mourned him as a friend as well as shipmate.

On the morning of the fourth of July, Mr. Carter wished to call and see a friend who was sick on the hospital ship *Valpariso* and asked Barney Doyle and me to pull the dinghy over there for him. We left the landing stage of the *Valpariso* to return a few minutes before noon, and were just abreast of the flagship *Wabash* and less than a hundred yards distant from her when eight bells struck and her battery broke loose with a National Salute of twenty-one guns. Such a pandemonium as roared about us for a few minutes I never expect to hear again. A salute heard from a distance of a half-mile or so is enjoyable; it can hardly be considered so when one is right under the muzzles of the guns and less than a hundred yards distant from them!

We were coaling ship on the 4th and a large coal-schooner was made fast alongside. In the afternoon we boys asked permission to go on board the schooner and visit her captain who was sitting on his quarter-deck. While we were all sitting there chatting, George Patterson bantered me to go aloft to the crosstrees with him. Knowing that I was green, he supposed I would funk. Having the captain's permission, we scrambled to the railing, one on each side, and I reached the main crosstree ahead of George.

After we had sat on the crosstrees enjoying the fine view over the harbor a little while, I banted George to shin up to the masthead and then slide down the stay to the fore-crosstrees, George demurred a bit, but finally said that if I would lead he would follow, I climbed up to the truck, swung one leg over the stay, took a good hold of it with both hands, and slowly slid down to the fore-crosstrees. George climbed to the main truck, just as I had done, but his courage failed and he slid back to the crosstrees again.

The captain of the schooner let out a volley of chaffing at George and told him he'd never be a sailor. Then he began upon me and told me I didn't dare climb to the fore truck and slide down the fore-stay to the end of the jibboom. It didn't look to be a very dangerous stunt to me, so I went to the fore truck, swung one leg over the long stay, got a good hold with my hands and began to slide. When about half way down, Mr. Ricker, who was officer of the deck on the *Nahant* at the time, happened to spy me and he called out a warning to me to "Look out"! Assuring him that I felt perfectly safe I released my leg from its turn over the stay and hung for a minute suspended by the grip of my two hands only.

It was "a fool-thing to do," as Mr. Ricker said when he had got me down onto the deck of the *Nahant* again. "It was just like a fool-boy!" Then he gave me a bully-good tongue-lashing, and ordered George and me to report to him on deck at eight bells that evening. "Here's where I get my first punishment," I said to myself, but when we reported to Mr. Ricker he had apparently thought better of the boyish prank. He gave us a good talking to, then told us to go below and turn in, and we heard nothing more about it.

The next day was Sunday, and in the afternoon three of us boys got leave, borrowed the dinghy, and pulled down to the ram *Atlanta*, which was anchored near the flagship. We were much surprised to find her in such a half-finished condition inside. The entire casemate deck was open from end to end, with only unbleached muslin partitions separating the quarters of the crew from the officers' wardroom aft, and there had manifestly been much haste in getting her ready for service.

The spar-torpedo-arm on the bow was manifestly a crude apparatus, and the elbow-like arrangement for lowering the spar into the water was a decidedly clumsy affair. A line from the trigger in the base of the torpedo was passed through three or four small staples set along the top of the spar and on into the box port, and a sharp pull upon this lanyard was to explode the torpedo at the right moment—if everything went just right! Whether such a clumsy apparatus could be successfully worked in the exciting moment of contact with an enemy vessel could only be told by trying, but that spar-torpedo certainly didn't look to be very dangerous to us after we had examined it carefully.

The powerful guns within the casemate did look dangerous; they were by all odds the finest guns we had ever seen, and we expended a lot of admiration on them. Why the ram didn't use those splendid guns upon the *Weehawken* as she was slowly approaching was most puzzling. We boys concluded that the officers of the *Atlanta* had been "badly rattled"!

The large hole in the side of the casemate, made by the XV-inch shot fired by the *Weehawken*, excited great interest. It was the first shot-hole punched through the side of a vessel that any of us had ever seen. It was so clearly punched through the iron armor and wood backing, it seemed as though the shop itself must have passed clear through. The hole certainly looked as though a XV-inch shot had penetrated there. Looking out through the hole, the innumerable splinters, all pointing inward, were much in evidence, and we could easily understand how the flying splinters from such a shot-hole as that had wounded and torn so many of the *Atlanta*'s crew.

The next day I was walking aft beyond the turret when my attention was attracted to a middle-aged darky sitting in a dugout canoe, who was beckoning me to come and speak to him by a peculiar crooking of his fore finger. I knew I had spoken with him before, and then recognized him as a man who had asked about our attack upon Fort Sumter soon after that event. He had said to me: "You-uns got badly whopped up there, didn't yer?" And I had acknowledged that we had got "badly whopped." He now asked me: "is you-uns goin' to win the wah, for shore?" I told him that we certainly believed we were going to win. "And will us niggers be free if you-uns win the wah?" he asked. I told him that he would be free, that all the negroes in the United States would be free, if the North won.

He looked at my face very earnestly for a minute or two, probably to assure himself that he wasn't being fooled, then he lifted a bit of white cotton cloth which was covering something in the bottom of the canoe and revealed a tin plate bearing a dozen or fifteen nice peaches, the first peaches I had ever seen. Selecting a beauty he passed it up to me, saying: "Youse good to us niggers, Massa!" I begged him to sell me the whole plateful of peaches, and told him I'd give him a quarter for them. He assented, and I went below to get the money, but when I got back to the deck I found that Mr. Carter had bought the peaches and sent them down to be placed upon the wardroom table, so the one the darkey had given me was the only one of them I had.

There had been several conflicting orders sent to Admiral Du Pont at the time of the failure of our attack upon Fort Sumter, and dissatisfaction with the results attained was implied if not directly expressed, the final result of the correspondence being that the Admiral suggested to the Secretary of the Navy that he be relieved and another officer be placed in command of the South Atlantic Squadron. This, however, wasn't such an easy thing for the Department to do, since there was a scarcity of able commanders of fleets at that time. [David G.] Farragut seemed to be the right man in the right place in the Gulf, and [David D.] Porter couldn't well be spared from the western rivers. After some time Rear-Admiral [John A.] Dahlgren was assigned to relieve Du Pont and had arrived in Port Royal early in July. On the morning of July 4th the flag of Admiral Du Pont was hauled down and that of Admiral Dahlgren hoisted in its place, and on July 6, Admiral Du Pont sailed for the North.

10 ‖ THE ATTACK OF THE ARMY AND NAVY UPON MORRIS ISLAND

I T WAS WELL UNDERSTOOD THROUGHOUT THE FLEET THAT ANOTHER attack was to be made upon Charleston, and that this attack was to be a joint effort of the Army and Navy. General [Quincy Adams] Gillmore, who had besieged and captured Fort Pulaski at the mouth of the Savannah River during the winter, was placed in command of the Union forces in South Carolina, and preparations for an advance had been made by erecting batteries on the northern end of Folly Island, which is separated from Morris Island by a tidal estuary called Light House Inlet.

Morris Island is about four miles long, Cumming's Point at the northern end being but about half a mile distant from Fort Sumter. The northern two-thirds of the island is comparatively flat, and about a mile of the northern end is narrowed by salt marshes and tidal creeks which make into the marshes from the harbor. A sand battery called Battery Gregg had been erected near the northern end of the island as an out-work of Fort Sumter, and a little later a second and larger battery called Battery Wagner was erected at the narrowest part of the island, some three-fourths of a mile south of Battery Gregg. This battery was later extended and much strengthened, and became the strong earth-work known to the Union troops as Fort Wagner, although the Confederates always used the original name of Battery Wagner.

The southern third of Morris Island was much broader, and there was a range of low sand-hills, the tops of which were thirty to forty

95

feet above tide water extending for perhaps three-fourths of a mile along the shore of the southern end. The Confederates had erected batteries mounting eleven guns and mortars upon the sand-hills nearest Light House Inlet and overlooking the northern end of Folly Island, and had prepared rifle-pits (or trenches) from which to oppose any attempted landing of troops from boats. General [Israel] Vodges was in immediate command of the Union troops on Folly Island, and he had erected batteries just south of Light House Inlet in which he had mounted forty-seven guns and mortars. These batteries were screened from the view of the Confederates on Morris Island by a fringe of small trees and bushes. Late in June Admiral Du Pont had been informed that the land forces were all ready to proceed with the attack, but as he was expecting to be relieved from his command, he asked that the attack be delayed a few days until his successor should arrive. . . .

When Admiral Dahlgren took over the command of the South Atlantic Squadron on the 4th of July 1863, he was shown a letter from General Gillmore to the effect that he was all ready to proceed with the attack upon Morris Island and asking the cooperation of the navy. Captain Ammen's *The Atlantic Coast* says:

> General Gillmore had informed him (Dahlgren) that the enemy appeared to be aware of his design, and was working on Morris Island with great activity to defeat it, and would succeed unless speedy action was taken. There being no time to ascertain the views of the Department it only remained for him to furnish the assistance required.
> This he proposed to do with the monitors, with what assistance from the wooden vessels was found practicable. He regretted the probability that at the time desired the *Ironsides* would not be able to cross the bar. He. says: "Of course, the most that is expected, from the action of these vessels is to relieve the troops as much as possible, and it is to be considered of no other consequence."[1]

Admiral Dahlgren at once proceeded to make himself acquainted with the vessels of his fleet, especially with the monitors, which he proposed to use in the attack upon Morris Island. I find mention in my diary that he came on board the *Nahant* on the afternoon of July 5th, and it was talked about among the officers in the wardroom that he

---

1. Ammen, 125.

made particular inquiry as to the fighting condition of that vessel and the health of officers and men.

It was ordered that the *Nahant* be got ready for sea as quickly as possible, and the next three days were certainly busy ones for us. Stores of all kinds, especially of shells and other ammunition, were taken in until our magazines and storerooms would hold no more, and late in the afternoon of July 8th we steamed out of Port Royal harbor and turned north. The next norning we came to anchor among the vessels on blockading duty off Charleston, just about where we had first anchored before our attack upon Fort Sumter in April.

The physical weakness which had so frequently manifested itself among both officers and men of our crew was cause for grave anxiety. The heat of mid-summer and the extremely bad air below-deck were the conspicuous causes of the frequent cases of sickness reported. Numbers of the men had been sent away to other vessels from time to time, their places being filled by drafts of fresh men from the receiving ship *Vermont*.

The day before we left Port Royal, 1st Assistant Engineer Bordley was condemned by a medical survey and ordered north to the naval hospital at Baltimore, and on the voyage up to Charleston, 3rd Assistant Engineer Neal collapsed while on duty in the engine room, and was the next day sent on board the gunboat *Powhatan* on sick leave.

In spite of the fact that we boys had been much in the open air during our two weeks in Port Royal and I had enjoyed much liberty, I was a good deal debilitated when we left for Charleston, and a severe attack of seasickness on the voyage up left me feeling decidedly ill. When I answered the sick call by appearing at the dispensary door on the morning of July 8 Doctor Stedman said to me:

"I've been expecting this! The fact is you are not strong enough to stand the strain on these poorly ventilated ironclads."

I strongly protested that I'd never been sick before, that I always spent a good deal of time in the open air, and that I *didn't* want to be sent away just as we were going into another fight. The doctor said: "Well, we'll see," gave me some medicine, and ordered me to report at the dispensary three times during the day for further doses, and told me to come to see him the next morning. Then he turned to the next case that was waiting. I had occasionally watched the more-or-less-sick men who came to the dispensary door at morning sick-call, but this was the first time I had felt the need of treatment since the *Nahant* had been put in commission.

At three o'clock on the morning of July 10 the call of "All Hands" was sounded. Breakfast was hurriedly prepared and as hurriedly eaten, and soon after half-past-four the anchor was hoisted and we got underway. Four monitors, the *Catskill, Montauk, Nahant,* and *Weehawken,* steamed in over the bar—the *Catskill,* from which the Admiral's flag was flying, taking the lead. Admiral Dahlgren desired to see for himself how the monitors behaved in battle, and chose the *Catskill* to be his flagship for the day.

We steamed directly in towards Fort Sumter and when about a mile from the shore of Morris Island we turned south towards Light House Inlet. It was a beautiful summer morning. The sun was rising behind us as we steamed in over the bar, and the clear morning light revealed to us the earth-works on top of the sand-hills at the southern end of Morris Island. These we well knew were our point of attack.

Upon the northern end of Folly Island, across the Inlet, I could clearly see a fringe of green trees and bushes, and quartermaster Bickford told me that fringe of green concealed the Union batteries. Even as I was gazing at it, I saw the row of greenery fall forward and a second or two later the flash of a gun was seen, followed in a few seconds by an upheaval of sand and a puff of smoke from the top of a sand-hill on Morris Island. The Union gunners had scored a fair hit with the very first shell they fired. It had exploded just upon the parapet of one of the Confederate batteries, and the battle was on.

It was some little time before the Confederates rallied to reply to the rain of shells from the Union batteries, at least it seemed quite some time to those of us who were watching the proceedings from our vantage point off shore. The monitors were so slow and clumsy in their movements, it was more than half an hour after the fight was opened by the Union guns before we were up near enough to open fire, and during that half-hour we were treated to the rare spectacle of a bombardment seen at comparatively short range.

The practice of the Union gunners was remarkably accurate and the summits of those sand-hills were belching puffs of sand and the smoke of bursting shells every second. Those sand-hill batteries were certainly a most uncomfortable position to hold once the Union gunners had steadied to their work. The Confederates did the best they could after they finally got to work, but it looked to us to be a decidedly unequal struggle. One of our officers who was watching the tops of the sand-hills through a glass, remarked that the Union guns were firing five shots to the Confederates' one. We did not know until many years afterward that the Union batteries mounted about four guns (and mortars) to the Confederates' one.

The four monitors gradually drew in towards the shore and we were called to quarters. In a few minutes the guns spoke out, and the monitors began dropping their huge shells upon the tops of the sand-hill batteries, taking them in flank and reverse. This bombardment by the guns of both the army and navy continued for about two hours and was extremely severe. The return fire of the Confederates was decidedly irregular, and was practically of no effect because of the perfect "rain" of shells from the Union guns. Some of the Confederate guns were dismounted and the soldiers manning them suffered severely.

A large fleet of launches, row-boats, and barges had been collected on the shore of a creek in rear of Folly island, well back within Light House Inlet, and about two thousand men of General [George C.] Strong's brigade were embarked in them. These boats now pulled out into the Inlet and made a dash for the shore of Morris Island. Such of the Confederate guns as could be brought to bear were turned upon this flotilla and one of the boats was sunk. The infantry occupying the rifle-pits did what little they could to prevent or retard a landing, but the shore was soon gained, the rifle-pits and batteries were carried with a rush, and the surviving Confederates made their way up the island as rapidly as possible in retreat.

The extreme heat of the day coupled with the loose sand made the retreat very difficult, and was equally hard upon the pursuing forces. About 150 wounded or exhausted men were captured by the Union troops, and the Confederates suffered a loss all told of about 300 that were killed, wounded or missing, out of a total force of about 700 men on the lower end of Morris Island that morning.

As soon as it was seen that the Confederates were retreating up the island, the monitors turned their bows north and steamed slowly along the shore, dropping a shell now and then into groups of Confederates when they could be seen beyond the low sand ridge near the shore. Captain Downes of the *Nahant*, apparently thinking that our work was done until we should draw near to Fort Wagner, ordered the hatches lifted off and that the crew be given a short recess in the open air, a respite which was much appreciated by the men, for it was stifling hot below.

When we boys reached the deck, the *Nahant* was quite near to and just a little outside of the *Weehawken*. A group of fleeing Confederates came into view for a minute through a gap in the sand ridge [and] the

Weehawken's XI-inch gun boomed out. I saw a huge shell sailing through the air, just touching the top of the sand ridge, and then exploding quite near the retreating soldiers. That great shell looked to be as large as a full moon as it sailed over the sand ridge.

We hurried below again as the call to quarters was sounded, and the *Nahant* steamed slowly along in the wake of the *Catskill*. In a little while we came under the fire of the guns of Fort Wagner and those guns brought to a halt the Union troops which were pursuing the retreating Confederates.

The four monitors dropped their anchors as near the shore as they could be safely brought (the shallow water along that shore of Morris Island made it very hazardous for us to come close in). It was the desire of Admiral Dahlgren to bring the monitors up to within grape-shot range of Fort Wagner, but this could not be done. The *Catskill* anchored at about 1,200 yards distance, and the *Nahant*, which was the fourth in line, was anchored about 1,800 yards from the fort.

It was about 9:30 o'clock when we anchored, and a steady fire of shells was kept up till noon. We then withdrew a short distance to give the men a breathing space and time for dinner. After a short rest and eating dinner, we returned to the attack and kept up a steady shelling of the fort until six o'clock, when we drew off for the night. The crews of the monitors had been at work with the guns for about fourteen hours; the day had been extremely hot and the men were thoroughly worn out.

There had been a light breeze from off shore during the day, but this had increased the discomfort of those of us who were below because it had blown the smoke from the guns back into the turret and it was drawn down by the ventilating blowers and distributed through the forward part of the ship. The air on the berthdeck was so thick with smoke at times we could scarcely see to do our work, and when we had a few minutes' leisure we lay prostrate on the deck in order to breathe the fresher air there.

Of this day's operations Captain Ammen says:

> Five hundred and thirty-shell and shrapnel were fired during the day, and from the different points of view the practice appeared to be excellent.
> The Admiral was favorably impressed with the endurance of the monitors. The *Catskill* was struck sixty times, a large percentage of the hits being very severe. The pilot-house, turret and side armor, were all more or less damaged. Some of the

shots were large; one found on deck after striking the turret proved to be X-inch; when these heavy shot struck, the concussion was very great. An officer touching the turret at such a time was knocked down senseless and much injured. The iron of the pilot-house was broken through entirely, and a nut from one of the bolts driven against the lining so as to break it through. The deck-plates were also cut through in many places, so as to make the entrance of water troublesome. The test was most severe, as all admitted who saw the vessel. Yet, after firing one hundred and twenty-eight rounds she came out of action in good working order, as was proved by her going into action the next day.[2]

A foot-note in Captain Ammen's book states that the above is a transcript from the official report of the Admiral, and then goes on to quote from the report of Captain Rodgers of the *Catskill* as follows:

The deck has been entirely broken through in four places, two of these sufficiently large to admit large quantities of water, requiring shot-plugs.———The hull was struck upon the port quarter, completely shattering all the plates. Two engineers and several firemen were prostrated by the intense heat in the fire-and-engine-room.[3]

Very naturally, because she was the flagship, the enemy had directed his fire almost wholly against the *Catskill*. The *Nahant* received six hits during the day, the *Montauk* two, and the *Weehawken* was untouched.

The next morning Admiral Dahlgren received a note from General Gillmore, telling that his men had made an assault upon Fort Wagner at daybreak, had been repulsed, and asking that the monitors take action to prevent reinforcements, which he had learned the enemy expected, from reaching the fort.[4] In accordance with this request the four monitors were again moved up to near Fort Wagner, and scoured the ground in rear of it with shells and shrapnel.

Of this early-morning assault upon Fort Wagner, Johnson's *Defence of Charleston Harbor* says:

The shattered and exhausted companies [of Confederates] reached Fort Wagner in a very disorganized condition which

2. This passage from Ammen (p. 126–27) is, in fact, a very close paraphrase of Du Pont's original report. See Du Pont to Welles, 12 July 1863. ORN, I, 14:320–21.
3. Ammen, 127n. The original letter is Rodgers to Dahlgren, 10 July 1863. ORN, I, 14:322.
4. See reference to this note in Dahlgren to Gillmore, 11 July 1863. ORN, I, 14:319.

lasted late into the night. And if an assault had been made that evening the whole island might have fallen. The Union army certainly lost a great opportunity.

About midnight fresh troops were brought from Charleston, particularly the Georgians, and a more determined spirit prevailed at once. The repulse inflicted on the enemy the next morning served to encourage the defenders of Morris Island and to confirm the purpose of the commanding general to hold it as long as possible.[5]

In the happenings of that night and the early morning of July 11, however, I was not interested. I was "down and out" before the close of the long hard day of July 10, begged to be excused from duty in the wardroom that evening, which time I passed lying upon the top of the turret enjoying the pleasant summer-night breeze over the water, and the next morning, in company of three men from the fire-room who had broken down from the excessive heat, I was transferred to the gunboat *Paul Jones* and the next day was passed on to the frigate *Wabash*, which was lying at anchor just outside the bar.

5. Johnson, 98.

11 ‖ Three Weeks' Sick Leave

The Assault upon Fort Wagner and Death of Colonel Shaw

The Adventures of the *Nahant*

The *Wabash* was a first-class steam frigate, the flagship of the South Atlantic Blockading Squadron, and was as clean and neat as the proverbial man-o-war.[1] An excursion around her several decks was a delight, after the dark and gloomy 'tweendecks of one of the monitors, and revealed the full meaning of the phrase, "Man-o'war fashion!"

At the time I was sent on board the *Wabash* (July 12, 1863), she was only about half manned, as many of her officers and men had been detailed to duty on other vessels of the squadron. The South Atlantic Squadron was quite short-handed and the less active vessels were partly stripped of men to make up full crews on board the more active vessels of the fleet. As the *Wabash* was very large and too unweildy for making quick dashes after intending blockade runners, she lay at anchor just outside the bar and could make-shift with fewer men.

That she was short-handed was of substantial advantage to the fifty or more invalids who were on board. Some two-thirds of the length of the gun deck had been stripped of mess tables, etc., and turned over to us for our exclusive use. We would spread down our hammocks and mattresses on selected sunny spots near the portholes and lounge there to our hearts' content. There was a "sick bay", of

1. The *Wabash* served as Dahlgren's flagship during his tenure as commander of the South Atlantic Blockading Squadron. It was an unarmored steam frigate built in the 1850s and carried forty guns of eight, nine, and ten inches mounted in broadside.

course, for those who were decidedly sick and in need of frequent attention from nurses, but for those of us who were simply broken down and chiefly in need of good food, sunlight, and fresh air, the freedom of the gundeck of the *Wabash* was a great boon.

And how "clean" she was! Her decks were as white as regular holystoning could make them; all the interior woodwork was white and had the appearance of being freshly painted. The guns and gun-carriages were jet black, with their brass-work cleaned and polished every morning, and every rope was symmetrically coiled in place. It is not at all strange that she seemed to me to be a very paradise of a ship.

It was early in the day when we were put on board the *Wabash* and I reported at the sick bay at morning sick-call. An attentive young surgeon took me in hand, looked at my tongue, felt my pulse and thumped me in the usual manner, then smiled at me and said: "You're not *sick!*"

"I know that, Sir," I replied. "I'm just broken down!"

"We can fix you up in short order," he went on. Then calling to an assistant, he ordered that I be put on the extra-good rations provided for convalescents, and that my hammock be spread down in a sunny location on the gundeck, and told me to just lounge there. "Take it easy," he said to me. "Live in the sunshine and fresh air, eat a lot, and come here to see me every morning." Not a bit of medicine did he give me except a tonic to stimulate my appetite, and I was left wholly to myself.

And what delightful days and nights those were. Unlimited sunshine all day long, and those were the long summer days, with the gentle sea-breeze drawing through the open ports, and "every prospect pleasing!" Not quite that, however. As I was sitting in a porthole on the port side and languidly watching the sunset tints in the west on that first evening, I was dismayed (and depressed) by the sight of the *Nahant* steaming out the channel opposite Light House Inlet and then turning away to the south. Each monitor had a distinctive band (or bands) painted around the top of her smokestack, so that it was easy to identify them at a considerable distance, and my heart sank as I saw the *Nahant* steaming away to the south and I not on board her, and I wondered if I was wholly separated from her. A day or two later I learned that she had again been ordered to Wassaw Sound because of reports that another ironclad ram had been fitted out at Savannah and would soon be coming out.

A long night's sleep (I had turned in at eight bells), quite restored my naturally buoyant spirits, and I lay in my hammock the next morning watching the sunrise tints glowing in the east with the feeling that I was very comfortable, and that the best thing for me to do was get myself well and strong again.

And there followed long, long days of rest and recouperation, with long nights of refreshing sleep. The friendly doctor smiled at me when I reported at the dispensary each morning: "Fine, fine!" he said. "You're coming on nicely. Just keep right on as you are going and we'll soon have you well."

When I mentioned to him one morning that I was troubled by the disappearance of the *Nahant*, and was wondering if I was ever to get back to her again, he suggested that I had better not go back to her, but would be better off if I would accept a transfer to the *Wabash*. "We are short a boy in the wardroom here," he said. "You'd much better stay aboard here with us than go back to that 'stuffy' monitor. If you do go back to her you'll almost certainly break down again." I told him I had shipped especially for service on the *Nahant*, and that I'd probably be homesick on any other ship. I also told him about the hard time I had had getting into the navy at all, that all my friends were on board the *Nahant*, and besides, she was *a fighting ship* and I loved her!

The doctor respected my attachment to my own ship, and told me he felt certain I could be sent back to her in due time. "I wish you'd stay on the *Wabash*, though," he said. "I'd like to have you for one of our wardroom boys. I thanked him for his kindness, but held firm to my desire to go back aboard the *Nahant*.

The first three days that I spent on board the *Wabash* I felt pretty weak, then I began to notice a decided gain. After that, each day's entry in my diary contained not only a record of the doings of the different vessels of the fleet, which were daily hammering away at Fort Wagner, but also the magic words: "Feeling better."

On the 15th of July the tide had been sufficiently high to permit the *Ironsides* to cross the bar. Thereafter she was on duty with the other ironclads, and her powerful battery was a substantial help. One difficulty was that she drew so much more water than the monitors, in consequence of her greater draft she could not venture near the fort because of the shoal water.

General Gillmore's men had been steadily pushing their batteries nearer and nearer to Fort Wagner, and keeping up a constant fire of shells upon the south face of that work. The monitors were steadily pounding the sea face, and besides the ironclads several of the wooden gunboats which mounted one or two long-range rifled guns could venture near enough to bring those to bear, firing over the ironclads. The bombardment of the fort went on daily, and it was my custom to watch it from the vantage point of a seat in one of the portholes of the *Wabash*, especially during the afternoons when the sun would be shining on the shoreward side of the ship, and always there was the feeling of regret that I wasn't on board one of those fighting ships.

On the morning of July 18, the doctor gave me a quite thorough going over, then he said: "If you still feel that you must go back to the *Nahant* I think I can start you on the way to her either this afternoon or tomorrow. You're in pretty good shape now, and with care I think you'll do." I thanked him and told him I'd be glad to start on the way to the *Nahant* at any time.

About mid-afternoon the tugboat *Dandelion* came alongside with half-a-dozen sick men to be put aboard, and the doctor's dispensary boy hunted me and said I was to go aboard the *Dandelion*. So a few "good byes" to the men and boys I had made acquaintance with, and I went over the side and down to the bobbing little tugboat. The huge frigate was as steady as a house in all ordinary weather, and the contrast between a great man-o'war and a little tugboat was a surprise. The *Dandelion* was fairly dancing upon the modest seas which the stately frigate noticed not at all. The doctor had bid me good by and good luck at the gangway, and I soon afterward found that he had especially commended me to the care of the captain of the tug.

Five wooden gunboats, five monitors, and the *Ironsides* had been steadily at work upon Fort Wagner during the day, their fire being especially heavy during the afternoon, and as we steamed in over the bar just before sunset, the roar of the great guns seemed to be well-nigh continuous. The captain of the *Dandelion* was a decidedly youthful naval officer and he had invited me to come into the pilot-house with him, and told me to make myself at home there.[2]

It was soon evident that something important was on foot, as regiments of troops could be seen formed on and near the beach south of the Union Batteries. The captain handed me a field glass to watch them with and told me the soldiers were going to assault Fort Wagner

2. The *Dandelion* was a small (90 ft.) steam tug. Its captain in 1863 was Acting Master C. Folsom, apparently no relation to Alvah. Hunter refers to the captain of the *Dandelion* as "Captain Blank" in the original manuscript. Presumably this is because sixty years after the fact when he wrote the narrative, he could not remember the young captain's name.

at dusk. As it grew dark the naval vessels withdrew, as the soldiers were then so well advanced there was danger in continuing the bombardment, and as the darkness deepened the troops moved forward to the assault. The *Dandelion* had steamed to a convenient anchor-buoy and tied up for the night. Captain Blank boosted himself to the top of the pilot-house, said: "Come on up!" and reached down his hand to assist me in the climb. From this vantage point we watched the advance of the troops until the deepening darkness hid them from our view.

The rapid flashes of musketry could be clearly seen and some of the rattle of it came to us over the water, the firing growing to be very rapid as the attack and defence got fully at work. After some little time it seemed that the attack was slackening, the firing grew less and gradually ceased excepting for an occasional flash from the rampart of the fort. "They have *failed!*" said Captain Folsom with a sigh, and after watching the shore through our glasses for some time longer we climbed down from the top of the pilot-house and turned in for the night.

The next morning we learned some of the details of the assault and heard that Col. Robert G. Shaw, of the 54th Massachusetts (Colored) Infantry, had been killed while leading his men. Later in the day we were told that a flag of truce had been sent to Fort Wagner in the morning with the request that Col. Shaw's body be given up to his friends, that it might be sent north for burial, and that the curt reply had been: "We buried him with his Niggers!"[3]

Johnson's *Defence of Charleston Harbor* tells that Confederate "General [William B.] Taliaferro had under his command at this time on the northern end of Morris Island about thirteen hundred men," of which number no doubt eleven hundred were in Fort Wagner where they could find protection from the Union shells in the capacious bombproofs. After describing several phases of the bombardment of that fort, and stating that the casualties were very few "and the injuries to the works no greater than could be easily repaired by the working-parties every night," the book tells:

> At length came the 18th day of July, made memorable by a land and naval bombardment of uncommon severity, lasting

3. On 18 July 1863 the 54th Massachusetts Infantry (Colored) spearheaded the land attack against Fort Wagner. According to tradition, the regimental commander, Colonel Robert Shaw, reached the top of the rebel position, yelled, "Onward Fifty-fourth," and was shot dead. His faith in the fighting capability of his black soldiers, and his heroism in the attack made him a martyr to the North.

eleven hours, and followed by the second assault of Wagner. This was bravely made, but stubbornly resisted, and it ended in a bloody and disastrous repulse of the Union forces.[4]

For three days I was the guest of Captain Blank on board the *Dandelion* and had much enjoyment in the constant activities of that little vessel as she went about her numerous duties: carrying messages, conveying men or supplies from one vessel to another, and making herself generally useful to the vessels of the fleet. At night I spread down my hammock on the floor of the pilot-house, with the windows and doors wide open, and during the days I passed most of my time there, sometimes even taking the wheel for a few minutes when the captain had a duty elsewhere. Those days and nights on board the *Dandelion* were very enjoyable chiefly because Captain Blank treated me with much kindness and did everything possible to make my visit pleasant.

On the afternoon of Tuesday, July 21st, we steamed alongside the monitor *Nantucket,* and I was sent on board that vessel with the information that she would, in due time, pass me on to the *Nahant.* There was need of another boy in the wardroom of the *Nantucket,* and I was given charge of three of the staterooms there, one of them being that of the Executive Officer and another that of the paymaster. This assignment to duty in the wardroom gave me the advantage of eating at the wardroom table after the officers had eaten. As I had no stated hammock location, I assumed the right of spreading down my hammock at night under the muzzle of the XI-inch gun in the turret, which gained for me good, fresh air to breathe.

The *Nantucket* proved to be a decidedly different vessel from the comparatively clean and tidy *Nahant.* The paint work of the berthdeck and wardroom had become a dingy gray from the frequent intrusion of powder smoke from the turret, the berthdeck was dark and damp, and there was a considerable heap of boat davits, oars, galley smokestack, etc. piled against the row of stanchions along the centre. On the *Nahant* all such things were stowed in a large storeroom opening out of the passageway leading aft to the fireroom, and the berthdeck was always clear and was kept clean.

The *Nantucket,* for some reason, didn't go into action along with the other monitors until July 24th, and I then quickly learned why she had so much powder smoke below. The ventilating blowers were kept running day and night but were stopped for a minute when the order

4. Johnson, 101.

was given to fire one of the guns. This stopping of the engines operating the blowers was a precaution against a possible accident to them which might be caused by the concussion of the gun. On the *Nahant* the men operating the engines started them up instantly the gun was discharged and the current of air thus moved carried the smoke upward and out of the turret. On the *Nantucket*, however, it might be two or three minutes before the blowers were started up again, and the smoke worked its way down below and throughout the ship.

On July 25th the monitor *Passaic* rejoined the fleet; she had been ordered north to Washington soon after our attack upon Fort Sumter in April. The next day the *Nantucket* steamed out over the bar about 3:30 o'clock in the afternoon and twenty-four hours later came to anchor in Port Royal harbor.

During the next four days we remained at Port Royal and I was twice on shore, once at Hilton Head and once at Bay Point. On one of the days that we lay at Port Royal I felt inclined to give the other wardroom boys one example of good work, so I thoroughly cleaned the paint and scrubbed the oil-cloth carpet on the floor of the Executive Officer's stateroom. So far as that stateroom was concerned, my effort was a complete success; the floor was clean, the paint was white and attractive in appearance, and the other officers looked at that room with envy.

The purser gave me two or three hints that he would be very greatly pleased to have his stateroom cleaned and brightened up, and other officers gave the other boys "hints" that they should follow the good example I had set them, but, they didn't *order* them to do it! I could see no good and sufficient reason why I should clean the purser's room since I was practically but a passenger on board, and no more cleaning had been done when, on August 1st, the *Nantucket* came to anchor in Wassaw Sound and a half-hour later I returned to the *Nahant*.

The officers of the *Nahant* had just finished supper when I went on board, and when I walked into the wardroom there was a splendid great sirloin-roast of beef upon the table flanked by a generous dish of roasted potatoes. A supply steamer had touched at Wassaw a day or two before and fresh meats and vegetables for the officers' and birth-deck messes were aplenty. While we boys were eating, I briefly told of my experiences while I had been away, then the boys told me of the adventures which the *Nahant* had passed through—and they were quite some adventures.

On both the eleventh and twelfth of July, Wagner had given the

Nahant a taste of its quality by heavy shot plowing three deep valleys in her deck, two of them so deep the woodwork beneath the plating was smashed down and the plating so badly broken that water passed through very freely. One of the hits was directly over the boilers, and if by chance another shot should strike the same spot it would most probably penetrate, so much was the deck weakened. Two heavy shots which struck the turret started a number of the bolts which held the iron plates together, and smashed the wooden shot-rack on the inside. Three shots had struck the armored part of the smokestack, two of them so heavy they had badly smashed the armor and disarranged the grating on the inside. This grating was to prevent a chance shell dropping down the smokestack upon the boilers.

When passing out the channel opposite Light House Inlet, the *Nahant* had struck quite heavily on the bar six or seven times, and for a few minutes the officers were apprehensive that she might ground there and be severely injured by the pounding, but she had kept up sufficient headway to slip over the bar and no serious injury was sustained. She had stopped at Port Royal for a day, and when they thought to proceed to Wassaw on the morning of July 14th so many men of the fire-and engine-room department were found to be unfit for duty, the ship could not go on her voyage till fresh men were obtained.

Four days after the *Nahant* reached Wassaw, the steamer *Memphis* brought to her a draft of forty-one men, which was more than half the total number of officers and men on board. What was probably of equal importance was the coming of two sets of submarine divers who went at once to work at cleaning the barnacles, etc. from the ship's bottom. This work went on for about two weeks, not being completed until after the ship was back in Port Royal.

The most exciting adventure (certainly for a brief time), had occurred on the night of the 22d of July. A little before midnight when everyone below was lost in the first heavy sleep, a muffled explosion was heard, immediately followed by shrieks and cries of men in great agony. Quartermaster Bickford, who was on watch on deck at the time, afterwards told me that before he had recovered from his surprise at the uproar below, Captain Downes sprang upon deck, with nothing on but his "nighty," his drawn sword in one hand and revolver in the other. Everyone had been apprehensive of a surprise-attack, for the *Nahant* was in enemy waters. Captain Downes' supposition was that his ship had been attacked by the enemy and he had hastened to the deck to do his utmost to repel boarders. The explosion, however, was found to have been on the berthdeck, and the cries were from men who had been sleeping in their hammocks.

It was found that one of the water tanks (which were about four feet square and set just beneath the berthdeck) was being filled from the condenser in the engine room, and the new fireman who was attending to that duty had not understood that the tank-cover should be left unfastened while the water was being pumped in. When he finally came forward to the berthdeck to see if the tank was full enough, steam was hissing from under the cover just as from the safety-valve of a locomotive.

The man tried to loosen the catch of the cover to let the steam escape, but it was firmly held by the pressure, so he struck the catch with a hammer which he had in his hand. This released the catch, the cover flew open and several gallons of scalding hot water was thrown upward by the pressure of the confined steam, part of it falling into the hammocks of the sleeping men. Seven or eight were scalded, most of them badly, but none fatally. All ultimately recovered. Curiously enough, the man whose ignorance caused the disaster escaped injury; he was behind the cover as it swung open upon its hinges and was thrown back out of harm's way.

While there in Wassaw Sound, the crew had been drilled regularly to train the new men, and two target-practice trips were made to the shore. Each afternoon half the men would be let go ashore for a fishing-swimming frolic with the seine, which gave them great sport in the warm water and usually resulted in a bushel or two of good fish for the messes.

Two deserters from the fortifications around Savannah had been discovered up-river in an old boat in which they made their escape, and they were brought to the *Nahant*. They were positively sure that the rumors of another ironclad ram being about ready to come down from Savannah were without foundation. Despite this comforting information, discipline was in no way relaxed. An armed boat was sent up-river on picket duty each evening, and every precaution was taken against a surprise-attack, which was what we had most to fear.

On August 2d the *Nahant* returned to Port Royal, leaving the *Nantucket* on blockade duty in Wassaw Sound.

12 || Repairing and Refitting

A Personal Difficulty

Fighting Forts Wagner and Sumter

A Torpedo Attack upon the *Ironsides*

The "Swamp Angel"

For ten busy days we remained at Port Royal having the damage to our deck and smokestack repaired, divers diligently scraping the ship's hull, store and amunition being replenished, and having massive base-rings put around the base of turret and pilot-house. These base-rings on turret and pilot-house were a device to strengthen the weak places there; they were expected to prevent such a welding together of turret and pilot-house as had put the *Nahant* out of business in the midst of the first attack on Fort Sumter, and to protect against a shot which might strike upon the angle where turret and deck joined, penetrating, and smashing the revolving gear of the turret.

The base-ring for the turret was about fifteen inches high by five inches thick, and came to us in five-foot sections. These were not joined together in any way but were simply bolted to the turret. The outer edge of the ring was rounded a little, and we boys found it made a very convenient seat if our feet were braced a little way out on the deck. The base-ring for the pilot-house was put on whole, being lowered down over the pilot-house from sturdy hoisting-sheers mounted on a flatboat, and it was an interesting performance to watch. After being lowered into place it was securely bolted to the wall of the pilot-house. On August 10 the coal bunkers were filled to capacity, and on the afternoon of the 12th we put out to sea. About four o'clock in the afternoon of the 13th we arrived off Charleston, crossed the bar as soon as the tide served and anchored with fleet of ironclads about a mile off Fort Wagner.

One advantage of getting back to the fleet headquarters was [the] opportunity to get our mail, quite a bag of which was brought to us next morning from the flagship, and this I had special cause to remember by reason of the trouble that came from it. In the mail was two copies of Harper's Weekly containing illustrations and descriptions of the Battle of Gettysburg; one paper to Mr. Ricker and the other to George Patterson. Of course, we had had the daily papers' reports of the battle three or four weeks before, but the pictures and detailed descriptions in Harper's Weekly were a great treat to us. We boys spent much time during the day studying George's paper, and I read aloud to them the descriptions of the battle.

We didn't know that Mr. Ricker also had a copy of that paper until he called me to his room just before he went on duty in the first dog watch, (four to six P.M.), and handed it to me, saying: "After you've looked it over all you care to, pass it out to the men on the berthdeck." I didn't think it necessary to tell him that George had a copy of that same paper, and I'd been reading it. But I looked his paper over for a time; then, it being time to set the table for supper, I took the paper out to Billy Wilson, and told him to pass it along to other men when he was through with it.

In some manner, George's copy of Harper's Weekly disappeared. We never could trace it, but a little while after we boys had finished supper, George came in from the berthdeck and went directly to Doctor Stedman with the tale that I had stolen his Harper's Weekly, and given it to Billy Wilson. Doctor Stedman was an intimate friend of Captain Downes and had served with him on the gunboat *Huron*. When the Captain and doctor were ordered to the *Nahant*, each had had his personal servants transferred also, and George considered himself as especially Doctor Stedman's boy, so [he] went to him with any grievance.

The doctor rightly thought such a complaint a serious matter, and took George to Mr. Harmony with it. Mr. Harmony listened to what the doctor had to say, then called me to give my version of the matter. I told him that Mr. Ricker had given me the copy of Harper's Weekly which I had given to Billy Wilson, and that Mr. Ricker had remarked that the paper had been sent him by his wife, and that, no doubt, it was a duplicate copy of the paper and not George's paper at all.

Mr. Ricker had turned in directly after coming off watch and eating his supper because he was to have the mid-watch that night, but he overheard the animated discussion in the wardroom, put on some clothes and came out of his stateroom to confirm my story, which, of course, exonerated me. It did not, however, satisfy George who went away looking as though he hated the whole lot of us. Possibly he really thought Mr. Ricker might be base enough to lie to shield me from punishment. I had charge of Mr. Ricker's stateroom, hence was "his boy", as we were called aboard ship.

After finishing my duties for the night, I got my cap and started to go on deck, putting on my cap as I passed through the door to the berthdeck. I had got two or three steps from the door when a crushing weight came down on my shoulders and back, bending me over nearly half way to the deck before I could gather myself together, and my cap was swept from my head by the swing of an arm which had aimed a blow at my face, but my half-bend forward had protected that.

Before I could straighten up to learn what was doing, I heard Mr. Harmony's voice roar out: "Mast'—'tarms! Put that d——d nigger in double irons in a coal bunker, and keep him there a week!" The master-at-arms already had George by the collar, having been close at hand and seen the attempt at assault, and it was the work of but a few seconds to put the "bracelets" on him and lead him away; the irons for his ankles were carried in the officer's hand to be put on after the coal bunker was reached.

It was easy to see that George had waited near the wardroom door until I should come out, bent upon revenging himself for the imagined wrong, and that Mr. Harmony had followed me onto the berthdeck because he mistrusted that George meant mischief. George's jumping upon my back as he struck at me had defeated his purpose, because his weight had bent me over so far his blow simply swept my cap off instead of giving me the "facer" that he intended. George still nourished his bitter feeling after he came out of the bunker. I asked him to shake hands and forget, but he sulkily refused, and there was never the same friendly spirit among the wardroom boys after the Harper's Weekly episode.

Following the disastrous assault upon Fort Wagner on July 18th, General Gillmore resorted to regular siege operations and approaches. His batteries were located for steady and severe pounding, and the approaches went steadily forward by zig-zags; this was a comparatively easy task in the soft sand of Morris Island. A severe fire of shells was kept up by his guns both day and night. The naval vessels kept at work upon the sea-face of the fort nearly every day. On some days the firing by the ships would be very severe and on other days few or no shells whatever would be fired from the fleet.

The objective of the descent upon Morris Island was the capture

or destruction of Fort Sumter. As the capture looked decidedly difficult, the destruction of that work was determined upon, and some
experimental shots were fired from Parrot rifled guns[1] located in
batteries that were six or eight hundred yards south and west of Fort
Wagner. The few trial shots revealed decided effectiveness in this fire
and satisfied General Gillmore that he could destroy Sumter from
where he was then located. Possibly the enemy would not hold Wagner
so stoutly once Sumter was well on the way to destruction! Special
batteries mounting heavy rifled guns were erected, the chief effort of
those guns to be the battering down of Sumter. One of those batteries
was manned by men from the frigate *Wabash* under the command of
Commander [Foxhall A.] Parker. These heavy rifled guns were
mounted at distances of 3,500 to 4,300 yards from Sumter and their
shots were directed at the gorge wall.

The "Gorge", so called, was the longest wall of Fort Sumter, and
as it was the land-ward (or Morris Island) face, hence in no danger
from the artillery of the time it was erected, it was less strongly built
than the walls facing upon the channel. This gorge wall was five feet
thick, built of brick, and was backed by arched casemates built of
brick. Immediately after the descent of the Union forces upon Morris
Island, it was suspected by the Confederates that an attempt might be
made to breach this wall, hence large working parties were set to
packing the casemates with wet cotton bales placed a few inches apart
and wet sand rammed into the spaces surrounding them, and this made
a solid wall seventeen feet in thickness.

When General Gillmore had all of his batteries completed, there
were eighteen long-range rifled guns mounted in them, and they were
capable of throwing a ton of metal at each discharge. Only about two-
thirds of the guns had been mounted, however, when the firing upon
Sumter began at five o'clock in the morning of August 17. The firing
was decidedly deliberate, it being the intention to make each shot score
a hit if possible. Also it was wise to not overheat the guns. By firing
each gun four or five times an hour, they could be kept comparatively
cool, and there was then less likelihood of a charge bursting them.

Four monitors, the *Ironsides,* and six wooden gunboats engaged

1. Named for its inventor, Robert P. Parrott, the Parrott gun was distinguished by its
single reinforcing band about the breech. The first such weapon was produced in 1860.
The reinforcing band was heated, so that it expanded slightly, then was slipped over the
breech which was kept cool by spraying the inside of the barrel with water. When the
band cooled, it clamped the gun barrel tightly and thus enabled the weapon to fire
heavier charges.

Fort Wagner on the morning of the 17th of August with the purpose of protecting the land batteries which were at work upon Sumter from the fire of the guns of Wagner. Admiral Dahlgren went in on the *Weehawken,* and after the tide had risen to nearly high water, the monitors were able to close in to within 450 to 500 yards of the fort and use grape and canister. The *Ironsides* drew considerably more water and could not safely be brought nearer than about 1,000 yards, but even at that range her powerful battery could do very effective work with shells. Before eight o'clock the guns of Wagner were silenced, after which the monitors and *Ironsides* fired less frequently.

A litle later the Admiral shifted his flag to the *Passaic* and, accompanied by the *Patapsco,* steamed up to within about 2,000 yards of Fort Sumter and opened fire upon the southeast face with a 150-pounder rifled gun from each of the two vessels. Sumter scarcely replied to this fire. Wagner had been silenced, and Battery Gregg, upon Cumming's Point, alone maintained the action on the Confederate side by occasionally firing a gun at one of the two monitors which had attacked Sumter. Fort Moultrie kept up a deliberate fire at the *Ironsides* scoring several fair hits.

About one o'clock the ironclads withdrew to give their crews a rest and time for dinner. After about an hour, the *Passaic* and *Patapsco* returned to the attack upon Fort Wagner to prevent the garrison of the fort working at repair of the damage done. Wagner fired a few shots at the monitors, but soon became silent again.

Early in the day a sad fatality had occurred on the *Catskill,* of which monitor Commander George W. Rodgers was temporarily in command at his own request. A heavy shot from Fort Wagner struck fairly upon the top of the pilot-house of the *Catskill,* smashing the iron plates down upon the heads of those on duty there, instantly killing Commander Rodgers and Paymaster Woodbury (who was on duty in the pilot-house as signalling officer) and wounding Mr. Peyton (pilot) and Master's Mate Wescott who was at the wheel. The *Catskill* temporarily withdrew from action and transferred the bodies to a tugboat, after which she resumed her position in the firing line. Commander Rodgers was Chief-of-Staff to the Admiral, and was a man and officer of the very best type. His loss was greatly deplored.[2]

2. George W. Rodgers was Dahlgren's Chief of Staff. He was the older brother of C. R. P. Rodgers, and a cousin of John Rodgers who commanded the *Weehawken* during the attack on Fort Sumter (see Chapter 6). For details of G. W. Rodgers's death, see ORN, I, 14:448–90.

At the close of this first day's bombardment of Fort Sumter, General Ripley, in command of the Confederate forces defending Charleston, reported: "Sumter in ruins and all guns on northwest face disabled, besides seven other guns."[3] Indeed, the Confederate officers had clearly seen that Sumter was doomed and they at once turned their attention to removing as many of the guns and as much war material as possible. This work was done chiefly at night. Of this first day's bombardment of Sumter, Johnson's *Defence of Charleston Harbor* says:

> The parapet of the gorge was for more than half its length demolished; the second and third stories of the western barracks, except a portion under cover of the gorge, were in ruins. Seven guns in barbette on the gorge, the left flank, and left face of the fort had been disabled. Some of the upper casemates of the left face had been damaged. During the day the garrison not on duty, as well as the working force of blackshad found safe shelter under cover of the gorge or within the splinter-proof blindage at its base.
>
> ⁂ ⁂ ⁂
>
> The total firing between 5 A.M. of the 17th and 5 A.M. of the 18th of August was 948 shots, of which 445 struck inside, 233 struck outside, and 270 passed over the fort.[4]

During the earlier firing upon Sumter with the smaller guns, [in an effort] to try the range of the Parrot rifles and determine whether Sumter could be effectively reached with them, one shell "passing over the western angle of the gorge and descending on the outside, struck the little steamboat *Hibben* then unloading at the new wharf. It penetrated the boiler, the steam scalding severely nine negroe laborers, some of them fatally."[5]

Fort Sumter was doomed—there was no doubt whatever about that after the destructive pounding it received on August 17, 1863. It was only a question of continuous pounding, but it withstood a tremendous amount of pounding between that date and the time of its ultimate evacuation by the Confederates. Fort Sumter was never "taken"; Charleston was not "taken" in the common acceptation of the term. It was only after being evacuated by the Confederates when

3. Ripley's official report was more sanguine. See Ripley to T. Jordan, 21 August 1863. ORN, I, 14:737–45.
4. Johnson, 120, 121.
5. Johnson, 116.

The results of the Union bombardment of Fort Sumter: (top) the interior of the fort; (bottom) an exterior photograph taken at the end of the war. (Cook Collection, Valentine Museum; National Archives)

118

General Sherman's army marched northward from Savannah in the winter of 1865, that they fell into the hands of the Union forces.

The bombardment of Sumter by the Morris Island batteries and the ironclad vessels went steadily on throughout the last half of the month of August, which was the period of "the first great bombardment of Sumter" as it was designated by Captain Johnson. This covered the time between the morning of August 17th and September 2d, and this great bombardment completely ruined Sumter so far as its being able to do any offensive or defensive work. At the end of this period there were still two or three guns precariously surmounting the shaky walls, but they were of no use to the defenders of the ruins. A Confederate flag was kept flying, but its sole purpose was to notify the Union forces that the ruins were still occupied by a small garrison that intended to defend them.

The firing upon Fort Wagner steadily continued both day and night from the land batteries, but the ironclads did very little firing at night because of the necessity of giving the crews time to rest. The men in the land batteries worked in three shifts, each gun's crew being given four hours' duty in the battery followed by eight hours back in the camp. This could not be done on the ironclads, however, because the entire ship's crew was on duty all the time it was in action.

The two weeks between August 17th and September 2d were strenuous ones for the ironclads because a determined effort was then made to restrict, so far as possible, the movements of working parties to and from Fort Sumter and the sending of relief parties to Morris Island. These movements were made in the night, and upon the ironclads devolved the duty of checking them if possible. Monitors were sent up-channel after nightfall to positions as near to Sumter as practicable, they withdrawing to their anchorage-buoys at the first hints of daybreak in the morning. The *Nahant* was on this picket duty four consecutive nights during the first week. As the crew was given the daytime for resting, we did no firing during those days.

Following the disaster to the pilot-house of the *Catskill*, it was thought best to re-enforce the tops of the pilot-houses on the monitors by coiling heavy anchor-chain upon them in such a manner [so that] the effect of a shot striking there would be chiefly expended upon the chain. The *Nahant's* pilot-house was so re-enforced on the 19th of August. On this day, also, George Patterson had gotten himself into trouble again by insolence to the master-at-arms. George had been released from confinement when we went into action or the morning of the 17th, and had been out of the coal bunker but two days when he was returned to it.

On the night of the 21st we were given a decided sensation in the shape of an attack upon the *Ironsides* by a small steam vessel equipped with a spar-torpedo. This little boat was commanded by a Captain [James] Carlin, who had run into Charleston some time before in command of a blockade runner and had there volunteered for this special service. The attack failed because the *Ironsides* was at the moment swinging with the tide and was bow-on to the torpedo boat when she approached. The Torpedo became entangled with the frigate's anchor chain, the armed sentries discovered the approach of an enemy and challenged with threats to fire, so Captain Carlin thought it wise to make his escape which he succeeded in doing in the darkness.[6]

On the night of the 23d all of the monitors were up-channel, and when within about 800 yards of Sumter opened fire doing considerable damage to the southeast face. Sumter replied with but six shots, but Moultire, with the powerful earthworks which flanked it, returned the fire with several heavy guns. Admiral Dahlgren was on the *Weehawken* that night and her pilot-house was struck twice, the Admiral reporting the blows from those two shots as being "more forcible than any he had seen."[7] The monitors withdrew about six o'clock in the morning, as a heavy gale had set in from the southeast.

On August 25th a very heavy bombardment of Wagner went on for some time and was interrupted by the coming out of a flag-of-truce boat with prisoners to be exchanged. Of this affair Confederate General Ripley reported:

> The enemy opened about daylight both from the fleet and land batteries. Wagner was sorely pressed, and the flag-of-truce boat was literally a godsend. The firing continued until 10 A.M., and for a portion of the time was equal in intensity to the bombardment of the 18th. One of the more advanced batteries of Parrot guns did serious damage; the remaining 10-inch columbiad on the sea face was dismounted, and the magazine so much exposed that it became necessary to remove the amunition. The commanding officer, anticipating a renewal of the bombardment

6. S. C. Rowan to Dahlgren, 28 August 1863. ORN, I, 14:497. See also the report of the commander of the Confederate torpedo boat, Carlin to Beauregard, 22 August 1863. ORN, I, 14:498–99.

7. Dahlgren to Welles, 23 August 1863. ORN, I, 14:502.

upon the completion of the exchange of prisoners, requested that all necessary arrangements be made for the transfer of the troops from the island in case of necessity. Four hours were consumed in effecting the delivery of 105 wounded prisoners and in receiving 39. The bombardment was not renewed, and the time thus allowed was improved to the utmost in repairing the damage done.[8]

There was an anecdote connected with the 10-inch columbiad mentioned above that is well worth narrating. That was the gun which did such execution upon the monitors such as breaking through the deck of the *Nahant* in three places on the 11th and 12th of July as previously told. This 10-inch gun was the last heavy gun mounted on the sea face of Wagner, a liberal reward was offered to any Union gunner who would put it out of business, and a number of gunners had attempted to dismount or destroy that gun. After three or four gunners on the *Ironsides* had tried to score on it and failed, an English gunner who claimed to have served on English men-of-war asked to be allowed to have a try at it. The gun could not be seen at all until it was run up to the parapet to be fired, and it disappeared from sight instantly it was fired; apparently it was mounted upon what we now know as a "disappearing gun carriage."

The English gunner was laughed at for asking to have a shot at the hated gun, but he carefully supervised the loading of his gun, took the lanyard in his hand and waited. The enemy-gun was seen to come up to the parapet of the fort, was discharged and disappeared. After ten or fifteen minutes it again appeared upon the parapet, was discharged and disappeared, and the gunner was hooted at for not taking his shot at it. He was carefully sighting his gun, however, and watching. After another considerable wait the enemy-gun was seen to be appearing above the parapet and the gunner instantly straightened up and pulled his lanyard. The enemy-gun disappeared from sight *without having been discharged* and a shout of triumph went up from those who had so scornfully hooted a little time before, for it was believed that the dreaded gun had been dismounted. This proved to be the case: the last heavy gun on the sea face of Fort Wagner had been dismounted by one

---

8. According to Ripley's official report, dated 22 September, the heavy bombardment and prisoner exchange took place on 23 August, not the 25th. Ripley reported that the cannonade on the 25th was relatively light and that "there were no casualties." ORA, I, 27:394–95.

of its trunnions being knocked off, and I sincerely hope the patient and successful gunner received the reward.

On August 28th a medical survey was held on board the *Nahant*, and both Captain Downes and Executive Officer Harmony were ordered north, sick; they left the next day. Lieutenant Commander [John J.] Cornwell was sent to take command of the *Nahant*, and Mr. Carter was given the additional duty of Executive Officer. Captain Cornwell felt that the rather modest salary of Lieutenant Commander did not warrant his keeping up a full establishment of cook, steward, and cabin boy, so [he] asked to join the wardroom mess at meals. This change made considerable difference to the wardroom boys as the new captain soon manifested a disinclination to get up to breakfast and ordered that that meal be served to him in his berth, a proceeding which distinctly lowered respect for the captain and weakened discipline among the crew.

In losing Captain Downes and Mr. Harmony, the *Nahant* lost two officers of the highest type. They were both "gentlemen" as well as officers, which is more than can truthfully be said of quite a few officers then serving in the South Atlantic Squadron. They were both capable and efficient, devoted to duty, and in Captain Downes' untimely death (which occurred in New Orleans about a year later, of yellow fever) the United States lost an officer it could ill spare. Mr. Harmony served in the navy for many years, rose to the rank of Rear Admiral, and I had the pleasure of renewing acquaintance with him when he was Chief of the Bureau of Yards and Docks at Washington.

On August 30th a new monitor, the *Lehigh*, arrived from the north and from this time on, it became the policy of the Admiral to have one monitor at a time sent down to Port Royal to refit and to give the crew a few days' rest from their arduous duties.

One other episode of this period should be mentioned, and that is the far-famed "Swamp Angel", which threw heavy shells into Charleston from a battery erected some distance out on the marsh. When the first great bombardment of Sumter began it occurred to some officers in the battery furthest west to try a few shots in the direction of Charleston. These shots so nearly reached the city, the officers were satisfied that they could reach Charleston if they could mount a gun a mile further west. The subject was much discussed, the marsh was explored, and a spot was found about three-quarters of a mile west of the left battery where it was believed a gun could be mounted if it could be brought to that spot, and the work was begun by constructing a causeway out there. The battery was erected, a 150-pounder Parrot rifled gun was brought to it and mounted, and on the night of August 21–22, fire was opened upon the city at a range of about 7,000 yards [with] the gun at an elevation of 35 degrees.

The result was entirely satisfactory. The city was reached by those 150-pounder shells and some damage done, but the gun burst at the 36th round and further effort in that direction was abandoned. After the war a Mr. Carr, an iron founder of Trenton, New Jersey, purchased the Swamp Angel along with a lot of condemned cannon, and being loath to melt down such an interesting relic, he united with a number of public-spirited citizens in erecting a pedestal upon which the gun was mounted as a monument.[9]

9. In the original manuscript, Hunter inserted here a passage from William S. Stryker's article on "The Swamp Angel" from *Battles and Leaders of the Civil War,* vol. 4: "Colonel Serell (the constructor) says that the distinctive features of the marsh battery as a work of engineering were "that the gun-platform was placed upon a gun-deck resting upon vertical sheet piling, outside and around which was a grillage of logs. If the gun and the other weights upon the gun-deck were heavy enough to tend to sink in the mud, the weight upon the grillage, in the form of sand bags, which formed the parapet and epaulement of the battery, by being increased, counterpoised the gun deck. It was simply a force meeting another force of a like amount in an opposite direction." The English journal *Engineering,* in its review of the Federal and Confederate armies at the close of the war, speaks of the construction of the battery as one of the most important engineering works done by either army. It was a successful piece of difficult engineering, and a practical method of inflicting damage on a city nearly five miles distant, regardless of its army, its cannon, and its great fortifications, which were within close sight and easy range."

13 | Fort Wagner Taken

The *Weehawken* Aground

A Naval Assault upon Fort Sumter.

W HEN I REJOINED THE *Nahant* EARLY IN AUGUST, I FOUND THAT several of the men had begun sleeping on deck, spreading down their hammocks at night just abaft the turret, and I at once joined the group. Now and then we would be driven below by the coming up of a sudden shower, or would be prevented from sleeping on deck by a storm or by a high wind blowing up such a sea that waves came over the deck, but the nights when we could sleep on deck in the mild summer air were most enjoyable.

Telling Barney Doyle of the great satisfaction it was to sleep in the open air induced him to try it, and after General Gillmore had pushed his batteries up close enough to make it worth while to keep the guns firing at Wagner all night, it was very real sport to turn in just as soon as we could get our hammocks, and lie with our heads bolstered up so that we could watch the shells hurtling through the air until they struck the parapet of the fort and exploded. Usually we would talk until some sleepy sailor near us would growl out: "Shut up, you youngsters, or I'll throw you both overboard!"

At first the shells from the Union batteries rose into the air somewhat as they made their curved flight towards Wagner, but later, when the light field guns had been advanced to within three or four hundred yards, the line of flight made by the sparks from the burning fuse would be almost level. From our position off shore and just abreast of the batteries, we would first see the quick flash of the gun, then, in a half-second, the light of the burning fuse, and could trace its flight by the sparks. If there were no fuse-sparks, we would know tht a solid shot had been fired, and towards the last nearly half the projectiles fired were solid shot because it was the general's plan to "shovel off" the top of the parapet of the fort until the bombproofs beneath would be no longer tenable, and solid shot were better than shells for that purpose.

There was also much pleasure in watching the mortar shells climb towards the sky, circle slowly over, and then down into Wagner. Those came from mortar batteries further back and the shells would revolve quite rapidly at first but when at the apex of their flight, the revolutions would be quite slow, then rapidly increasing as the shell gained momentum in its downward course. Now and then a shell would explode before it reached the fort and sometimes one would plump down into the sand, a muffled explosion soon following. The purpose of the constant firing at night was to prevent working parties in the fort from repairing the damage done during the day, and for hindrance of work exploding shells were more effective than solid shot.

The *Nahant* was given much picket duty at this time and there was, of course, no sleeping on deck when the ship was up-channel never Fort Sumter. We did manage to catch some sleep on those nights by those of us not on duty lying about on the berthdeck. On some nights about half of us would sleep four hours while the other half attended to the duties, then we would change places and those who had been on duty would sleep four hours.

The "approaches" to Fort Wagner had been pushed nearer and nearer, and the constant rain of shot and shell upon that work was supplemented by charges of grape and canister, the more effectively to smother the return-fire of the fort and retard the repair of damages. The ironclads assisted at the work as seemed desirable. For instance, the *Ironsides* steadily bombarded Wagner all day on September 5th, three monitors going in to her support towards evening. The four vessels continued their fire till midnight.

On Sunday, September 6th, all the ironclads went into action at seven o'clock in the morning and kept up their fire till 2:30 P.M. My diary tells: "Slept from 2:30 to 5:45 P.M., then firing at Wagner again until 10:30 P.M., when all came out except the *Ironsides*, she continued the action". On these two days and nights the batteries had redoubled their efforts, if that was possible. An incessant fire of shot, shell, grape and cannister [was] being thrown at the doomed fort all the time.

Of this terrific bombardment Johnson's *Defence* says:

General Gillmore decided to concentrate on Wagner the tremendous fire of one 10-inch rifle, four 8-inch rifles, nine 6-inch rifles, and ten 30-pounder rifles—in all twenty-four rifle-guns, together with seventeen mortars. These were to be supported by the powerful batteries of the *New Ironsides* and the other vessels of the armored squadron, adding to the land fire at least twenty more of the heaviest naval guns ever used in warfare. The grand total between sixty and seventy guns and mortars, against Wagner's twelve effective guns.

Accordingly, at daybreak on the morning of the 5th of September all of this artillery opened upon Fort Wagner, and in a short time silenced it. The garrison, about 900 men, could not stand to the guns, and betook itself to the best cover to be found. It is a mistake to suppose it was, as a whole, sheltered in the bombproof; hardly one-half could have endured the heat and crowding of those close quarters: a portion, about two hundred, were stationed without and to the rear in the low sandhills affording some natural cover. All that day and night, the day after and some part of the night following, the garrison, suffering considerable loss and constantly increasing discomforts almost as great as dangers, continued firm in its heroic fortitude under fire seldom if ever before equalled in severity, and certainly never before directed at so small an object. The land batteries threw 1663 rifle projectiles and 1553 mortar shells. The New Ironsides contributed 488 shells in the same time, and together with that of the monitors, the total fire must have been little short of 4,000 shots in forty-two hours. . . .

A calcium light stationed at the left of the second parallel was used by the attack with great success to illuminate the parapet and higher parts of Wagner, so as to deter from any effort at repairing damages of the day. It was hardly necessary. In the effort to repair damages on the night of the 5th, Colonel Keitt reported a loss in killed and wounded of sixty to eighty men of the working party alone. So plain was the crisis now become that Brigadier General Gillmore decided to assault the work at nine o'clock on the morning of the 7th, and all preparations were made for that end.

The sappers, though unmolested by the fire of the work itself, were made to suffer by the long-range fire of the flanking batteries on James Island until the approach became so near as to endanger the garrison. This period was reached when the sap was about to push by the south-face toward the close of the second day. Thence forward the sappers had nothing to fear, not even any longer the torpedoes; but, entirely under cover of the east, or sea-front, they advanced nearly to the flank of that front, where they finished their labors and entered the ditch about ten o'clock that night.[1]

The Confederate chief-engineer made an examination of the condition of Wagner on the evening of September 6th and advised immediate evacuation of a position which was no longer defensible. The evacuation of the fort and of Battery Gregg was immediately put in motion and so successfully carried out that the entire garrison [escaped] excepting two or three boats containing forty-six soldiers and sailors under Lieutenant Hasker which were captured by the Union pickets.

And Wagner was ours! Great was the rejoicing on the morning of September 7th, when it became known to the officers and men on the ironclads that Fort Wagner had been evacuated during the night and immediately occupied by General Gillmore's men. It had been a long and hard fight; we gave credit to the enemy for having put up a stout resistance. All the greater was our satisfaction at seeing the Stars and Stripes floating over the ramparts at which we had hurled so many shells and from which we had received in return some pretty hard knocks.

Johnson writes:

> Thus terminated the seige of Battery Wagner, memorable for its duration of forty-eight days, for the persevering skill displayed in the attack, and for the sturdy resistance of the defence. History will promote it from a battery to a fort, but it was always known to the Confederates as "Battery Wagner." In conjunction with Battery Gregg at Cumming's Point, it had repulsed three assaults of the enemy, and stood without any serious damage to the last one of the heaviest bombardments on record. . . . The highest compliments were paid to the commander of the Union forces by his superiors at Washington. And yet the Confederates were not without their satisfaction also in having made a stand for the defence of Charleston that availed them to the end of the war. For the conquest which they left to the enemy was fruitless; the barren island was but a barren trophy.[2]

Soon after Admiral Dahlgren knew that our troops held all of Morris Island, he sent in a flag of truce and demanded the surrender of

1. Johnson, 148–49, 150.
2. Johnson, 151–52.

Fort Sumter, receiving in reply the message: "Inform Admiral Dahlgren that he may have Fort Sumter when he can take and hold it."[3] The rear-admiral had informed General Gillmore, also the Secretary of the Navy, that if the demand was refused he intended to move at once upon the fort and obstructions with all of his ironclads, but this purpose seems to have been changed into a plan for a night-assault upon Fort Sumter by marines and sailors from the fleet conveyed in boats and launches.

This proposed assault was postponed for a couple of days because of the *Weehawken* accidentally running aground on a shoal near Fort Sumter. The tide was ebbing at the time and nothing could be done to release her from her dangerous position until high-water, late in the afternoon. As soon as it became known on board the other vessels that the *Weehawken* was aground and exposed to the fire of most of the guns on Sullivan's Island all the ironclads moved up and opened a furious fire upon Fort Moultrie and the batteries there. They ceased firing a little after seven o'clock, and all withdrew excepting the *Lehigh* and *Nahant*, which stood by the *Weehawken* through the night to assist or protect her.

It seems almost incomprehensible that the Confederates did not discover the plight of the *Weehawken* until the morning of the 8th, twenty-four hours after her accident. When they did discover it, they immediately opened fire upon her from a dozen heavy guns in Fort Moultrie and the adjacent batteries. The ironclads were already moving up to protect her and the firing from both fleet and forts became fast and furious. The *Weehawken* joined in most gallantly in spite or being at a serious disadvantage. At low water her hull was much exposed to the enemy's shots, and it is remarkable that she escaped serious injury from them.

Early in the afternoon, while swinging with the current at the change of tide, the *Patapsco* shot away a part of the armor of her own smokestack, in exactly the same manner the *Nahant* came so near doing when the ram *Atlanta* was coming down upon us as told in Chapter 8. The XV-inch guns on the monitor were sighted by the officers in command of them looking through peepholes set in the sides of the turrets three or four feet to the right of the gun, and they might not know it if the muzzle of the gun bore directly upon their side of the smokestack. On the *Nahant* this fact was discovered by the gunner

3. Quoted in Johnson, 156.

holding the lanyard and an accident to our smokestack was averted by his informing the officer of the danger. On the *Patapsco* it was not discovered, the gun was discharged, a section of the armored part of her smokestack was shot away. The smokestack at once tipped over so that it stood at nearly a right angle. This cut off the draft which kept up the fire in the furnaces, and she was disabled.

The *Nahant* being nearest to the *Patapsco* we passed her a line to attach to the end of her hawser, which we drew one end of to our smokestack and made it fast (we had no bitts) and then towed her out of the zone of fire and down to the anchorage. We then returned to again join in the action. Just as we reached the vicinity of the other monitors, the *Weehawken* was floated off the shoal and all the iron-clads withdrew. We fired both our guns at Fort Moultrie as a parting salute.

When we boys came on deck and took a look at Sullivan's Island, there were great clouds of dense black smoke rolling up from a large summer hotel and a village of cottages which stood in the rear of Fort Moultrie and the batteries on each flank of the fort. It was a most comforting sight, as it was good evidence of the efficacy of the Union shells and satisfied our boyish desire to see the results of our hard work.

Captain Johnson gives the following account of this effort of the ironclads to protect the *Weehawken* when that vessel was aground:

> Commander [Edmund R.] Colhoun [of the *Weehawken*] made a very gallant fight fight under all his disadvantages. . . . But his escape from destruction was due to the diversion made in his favor by the vessels of the squadron; for his monitor was hit twenty-four times, and the damages required sixteen days for repair; three of the crew were wounded; the vessel was got afloat again about 4 P.M.
>
> The diversion made by the rear-admiral to cover his endangered monitor began about 11 A.M., and led to what was probably the severest naval engagement in American History up to that time. the *New Ironsides*, together with the *Patapsco*, *Lehigh*, *Nahant*, *Montauk* and *Passaic*, came to anchor from 1,400 to 900 yards distant from Fort Moultrie, and for nearly three hours delivered by far the heaviest cannonade heard from the naval force off Charleston harbor. The Confederate works suffered no damage of much importance; of about thirty engaged, two guns were dismounted, and mainly, the casualties were those already mentioned in connection with one shell fired

by the *Weehawken*. The total number killed were 19, and wounded 27. . . .

To a looker-on from Fort Sumter that day the Federal navy seemed to have altogether the best of it; for the stranded monitor got off with flying colors, and the Confederate batteries appeared to be silenced more than once.[4]

Here I have to take issue with Captain Johnson's *Defence of Charleston Harbor*, and taking issue with him is all the harder because there is ample evidence of painstaking accuracy and absolute fairness to both sides throughout the book. Not only does the book itself give abundant evidence of accuracy and fairness, but in talks that I had with Mr. Johnson during a week's visit to Charleston some years ago, it was easy to sense the clarity of mind and high standard of honor which prompted his every statement. At the time of my visit to Charleston, formerly Captain (afterwards Major) Johnson was the rector of St. Philip's Church in that City, and he was a greatly beloved clergyman. His book states that the diversion made by the ironclads to cover the endangered *Weehawken* "began about 11 A.M." and continued "for nearly three hours". My diary distinctly records it thus: "Firing at Moultrie from 8:45 A.M. to 2:15 P.M., then the *Patapsco* became disabled. We got her hawser and towed her out of action. A lot of houses burning near and back of Moultrie. Went in again to help protect the Weehawken; she had got off. We fired both guns at Moultrie for spite".

It is perfectly clear in this statement that we began the diversion at 8:45 A.M., and it is certain the effort at diversion was continued till the *Weehawken* came afloat again from 4 P.M.—seven hours instead of Captain Johnson's "nearly three hours". The record, in my diary, which I have quoted verbatim, was made on the evening of the day on which the events occurred, and I am compelled to believe the time given is accurate. There certainly would be no reason for misstatement in a simple record of events of the day.

Captain Johnson was an officer of engineers in the Confederate army and was on duty *in Fort Sumter*. In the above quotation he speaks of himself as a "looker on from Fort Sumter" on this day. From the fact that his book was not written until many years later (the preface to it is dated December 1, 1889), I am induced to believe that he did not make record of this affair at the time, and that his mention of the beginning of

4. Johnson, 157–58.

the "diversification" and of its duration was made from memory, hence the error as to the hours.

In confirmation of the accuracy of my diary, I find that the official report of Colonel Butler, commanding the Confederate artillery forces on Sullivan's Island at this time, describes the discovery of the *Weehawken*'s being aground, and states:

> I directed a slow fire to be opened upon the monitor from the treble-banded Brooke gun and the X-inch columbiads, I think with some effect. The fire was returned, and about nine o'clock a.m. five other monitors, with the *Ironsides* were seen approaching; whether to shield the boat that was thought to be aground, or whether it was a preconcerted move, I am unable to say.[5]

That "about nine o'clock" is sufficiently near to my positive "8:45 A.M.", and as Col. Butler's report was probably written by his adjutant, it may be accepted as *fairly accurate* where absolute accuracy was unimportant. Incidentally, my mention that we "fired both guns at Moultrie for spite" is genuinely boyish.

In reporting this affair to the Navy Department Admiral Dahlgren wrote:

> Captain Colhoun has, in my opinion, more than compensated for the misfortune of getting aground by the handsome manner in which he has retorted on the adversary and defended the glorious flag which floats above him. At 11½ A.M. I telegraphed to him: 'Well done, *Weehawken!* Don't give up the ship.' We may lose the services of this vessel—I hope not—but the honor of the flag will be maintained.
>
> P.S. I am happy to say that at high water the *Weehawken* was gotten off. I commend Captain Colhoun, his officers, and crew to the notice of the Department. The crews of the other vessels cheered spontaneously as he passed.[6]

All of that day (September 8th) Admiral Dahlgren was busy with preparations for a naval assault upon Fort Sumter. Boats and launches were towed inside the bar from the vessels on blockade duty outside and assembled at a convenient place for embarking the sailors and marines that had volunteered for the service. A request was sent to

5. Col. W. Butler to Capt. Edward White (Asst. Adj. General), 12 September 1863. ORN, I, 14:577.
6. Dahlgren to Welles, 8 September 1863. ORN, I, 14:550.

General Gillmore asking that he loan a score of his boats and launches which brought the information that General Gillmore was himself planning an assault upon Sumter that night, and the army boats were assembled in Vincent's Creek, just in rear of Cumming's Point.

Lack of harmony seems to have characterized the efforts of the two branches of the service when a joint-attack by both the army and navy might have scored a brilliant success. The assembling of some two-score boats and launches was noted by the Confederates who knew at once that an assault was coming and prepared for it by reenforcing the garrison of Fort Sumter and bringing down from Charleston a supply of hand grenades and fire-balls.

The ironclads took no part in the assault, and my diary of September 9th simply states that: "A naval storming party tried to take Sumter last night and failed." Captain Ammen, in *The Atlantic Coast*, reports the attempt as follows:

> On the night of September 8th an attempt to take Sumter by a boat expedition from the squadron resulted disastrously, not in great loss of life, but in the capture of a considerable number of officers and sailors, as well as the loss of several boats. The demand for the surrender of Sumter had informed the enemy, and boats in tow of tugs from vessels outside the bar during the whole afternoon, left little doubt as to an intended attempt. He did not fail, therefore, to put a considerable force into Sumter for the occasion.
>
> Commander T. H. S. Stevens was in command, and Lieutenant-Commander E. P. Williams, Lieutenants Remey, Preston, Higginson, and Ensign Craven, commanded the five divisions of boats." A detachment of marines, under Captain McCawley, formed also a part of the force, numbering in all 400. A request for the loan of some army boats brought the information that General Gillmore also intended making an attack. It was about ten P.M. before the boats in tow of the tug reached the vicinity of Sumter; "A sound of musketry, followed by shells from the adjacent forts, announced the assault." Before the Admiral reached the vicinity the conflct had ceased. Of the 400, ten officers and 104 men were taken prisoners, and three were reported killed.
>
> The boats, on approaching the fort, were met with a fire of musketry, hand-grenades, lighted shells, and grape and cannister, and simultaneously, at a signal from the fort, all of the enemy's batteries, with one of their gunboats and a ram, opened fire.

Several of the boats effected a landing, "but the evidences of preparation were so apparent, and the impossibility of effecting a general landing or scaling the walls so certain, that orders were given to withdraw." All who landed were either killed or taken prisoners. They were, in fact, entirely helpless, and when they agreed to surrender were taken around to another face and helped to get into the fort.[7]

This attack appears to have been not only ill-advised, but to have been made without adequate preparation in the shape of reconnaissance to determine which was the best face of the fort to assault. Captain Johnson's *Defence* states that "the prisoners told Major Elliot that they scarcely expected any resistance." Then adds:

But the great mistake of the assault was in not attacking on the side of the gorge, where a practicable slope, though of a very rough footing would have favored them. Had two divisions of the boats made that their place of landing, or, better still for the Federals, had General Gillmore's assault with troops from Vincent's Creek, west of Cumming's Point, been made in concert with the naval attack, so that while the latter were occupying the garrison on the northern and eastern fronts, the former would have threatened the gorge, there might have been a very different result for the fort. As it was, the easy victory of the Confederates confirmed them in their resolution to hold their ground to the last. The repulse of this boat-attack was felt to be a reassuring event in the history of the fort, as well as a new honor worthily to be borne by its brave defenders.[8]

7. Ammen, 138–39.
8. Johnson, 163–64.

14 ‖ FINDING A FLOATING MINE

ANOTHER NIGHT ATTACK UPON THE *IRONSIDES*

Iℕ ᴛʜᴇ ᴡᴇᴇᴋꜱ ꜰᴏʟʟᴏᴡɪɴɢ ᴛʜᴇ ʜᴇᴀᴠʏ ꜰɪɢʜᴛɪɴɢ ᴏꜰ Sᴇᴘᴛᴇᴍʙᴇʀ 7ᴛʜ and 8th, the purpose of which was the protection of the *Weehawken* while she was aground within range of Fort Moultrie, there was little hard fighting by the ironclads of the South Atlantic Fleet. There was work enough to keep us busy, the most important being the night picket duty up-channel. The vigilant picketing of the channel leading to the inner harbor was kept up because of complaints which had reached Washington that extra-venturesome blockade runners were now and then succeeding in getting into or out of Charleston in spite of the blockading vessels outside the bar and the large fleet at anchor in the outer harbor.

That such should be the case is hardly surprising. There were three channels over the bar and into the outer harbor of Charleston, which merged into the one channel passing in between Forts Sumter and Moultrie, and a shrewd blockade-running captain could steal in close to the shore of Sullivan's Island a few miles up the coast, then by hugging the shore dangerously close, (in which he would be aided by a few signal lights flashed from the shore), he could succeed in running past the vessels blockading the northern (or Sullivan's Island) channel[1] and edging past the monitors picketing the main channel. The profits of blockade running were very great and it paid to take the chances.

The blockade runners did not always succeed in getting by, as an

1. Also known as Maffitt's Channel.

occasional burning wreck to be seen on the shore of Sullivan's Island attested. Now and then we would be startled out of sleep by the signal rockets and the flashes of guns on a blockader outside which had discovered a vessel attempting to steal in, and we would steam in as close to Sullivan's Island as the state of the tide would allow to be rewarded by seeing nothing unless, possibly, a light at a distance until the coming of day revealed a burning wreck three or four miles up the shore.

Captain Ammen in *The Atlantic Coast* states that at this time "The naval operations before Charleston were now only of blockade, and though the channel was certainly very limited the blockade-runners came and departed," but "The Navy Department was not informed of the fact." In a footnote he adds:

> The Secretary of the Navy appeared before the "Joint Committee on the conduct of the War" and assumed that because "the Department was not informed of the fact" no vessels ran the blockade; actually twenty-one vessels ran in after the ruin of Sumter until the evacuation of Charleston.[2]

On the morning of Sunday September 13th, we had quite a scare. I had taken the usual cup of coffee to the officer of the deck, Mr. Carter, that morning, and while he was sipping the coffee and eating the slice of bread and butter, I entertained myself by looking out over the water, more especially in-shore toward Morris Island. A black object slowly floating along on the outgoing tide attracted my attention, and I soon noted that it was gradually drifting towards the ship. If floating along with the tide only, it would have passed the *Nahant* at a distance of perhaps a hundred feet, but there was a gentle off-shore breeze and tiny waves and those tended to drift the floating object against the ship's side.

Calling Mr. Carter's attention to the object, I ventured the suggestion that it was some part of the much-feared "obstructions," and that it had got adrift and floated down into the outer harbor. Mr. Carter exclaimed: "It's a torpedo!" and called to one of the sentries to put a bullet into it, thinking to have it explode while it was still some distance from the ship. He changed his mind, however, before the sentry had fired at the object, stationed two men equipped with boat-hooks at the side to prevent the thing coming in contact with the ship,

2. Ammen, 141, 141n.

and sent the quartermaster to inform Captain Cornwall that a floating torpedo was drifting down toward us.

Just as the captain hurried on deck, the black object drifted near enough so that one of the men could secure the iron point of a boat-hook beneath a small rope, which we could see was netted about what had apparently been some kind of small cask, but had been lengthened. One of the men said it was a beer keg, but it was about three feet in length and had pointed ends. It eventually proved to a former beer keg which had had cone-shaped pieces of wood fitted into the ends, the wooden cones being probably intended to increase the buoyancy of the keg.

There was a small cupola-like projection secured above the bung-hole with screws, and this we found to be a metal base for a percussion fuse-plug, or some other kind of firing apparatus. There was what appeared to be a wooden plug set into the screw-threaded opening where we supposed the fuse-plug was to be fixed, and the whole was covered with a thin coating of tar.

Nearly everyone seemed to be in terror of our captive. Evidently Mr. Carter's having pronounced it a torpedo had convinced everyone that this unknown black object was a very dangerous neighbor, and all of the officers and men that had come on deck were grouped back of the turret, as far as possible from it, and where they were well protected from the effects of an explosion should an explosion result from our investigations.

Mr. Carter, who was both Executive Officer of the ship and officer of the deck at the time, was in charge of the situation. After the man who was holding the thing off from the ship's side by a boat-hook and I had studied it for a few minutes, I made bold to go to Mr. Carter and say that the thing was harmless and gave as a reason for my belief the fact that a wooden plug was occupying the place where a fuse-plug was intended to be placed, and that there was no way to fire any exploding charge if there *was* an exploding charge inside the thing.

This was an expremely "cheeky" thing for a boy to do, but I felt a sort of proprietary right in the torpedo (if it was a torpedo) since I had been the one to discover it, and I had not, up to that time, felt the fear of it that everybody else seemed to feel. My confidence, however, might well be a case of "A fool rushing in"! I had no knowledge whatever of explosives as such, and based my confidence on what I thought was "Mechanical instinct."

Doubtless, too, the confident assertion of the boat-hook man that they were "all fraid-cats!" and that the "beer keg" (as he called it) was harmless, had contributed to make me bold. At any rate after listening to the boat-hook man for a minute or two, I went back to Mr. Carter and suggested that a sling be put around the object, and that a boat-tackle be hitched to it, and we hoist it up to the boat davit. The fact that the man and I were just about 'midship with the object, and that a boat davit was standing a little way aft of us, probably gave me the idea.

Mr. Carter asked me, "Will *you* put a sling around it?" and asked it with an emphasis which implied a dare. I replied that I would if some of the men would hold a boat in such a position that I could work from the bow of it, and not endanger the ship by bringing the object up to the side. A couple of men volunteered to hold the boat, the 2d cutter was drawn forward so I could step into it, then was drawn up to the object and held between it and the side of the ship, so that I could lean down and work the sling over first one end and then the other. The boat was floated back to the boat davit, the fall-block-hook was reached out to me, and I set it into the bight of the sling and gave the word to haul taut. Then the boat was backed aft again and I regained the deck.

Two or three men had grasped the tackle to hoist, but Mr. Carter stopped them until he had directed me to take the boat-hook and hold the thing away from the ship's side, and I stood there keeping the supposed torpedo the length of the boat-hook-handle away from the hull while the men slowly hoisted it up to a height of about five feet from the water. As the object came up clear of the water, it could be seen that there was a rope made fast to the under side of it, and that the rope extended down out of sight in the water—but it was eight bells and breakfast time.

At eight bells Mr. Ricker had relieved Mr. Carter, and was in charge of the deck when I hurried up there again as soon as the officers were fairly well through breakfast. I went directly to the side near the suspended object to study it, and made out that there was a three-eighths-inch manilla rope netted around it, and that a doubled and slack-twisted section of the rope hung down into the water. This looked to be even more doubtful than had the floating object itself, because it suggested something mysterious and possibly dangerous at the other end. A small cluster of weights was secured to the under side of the keg, and those weights indicated to us that the keg was some kind of buoy to support the really dangerous "mine" which we supposed was at the other end of the rope.

Boy-like I took up one of the boat-hooks and began "feeling" of the rope down near the water, moved to investigate the thing by thinking I had seen the rope sway a little in the breeze that was blowing. Just at that moment Mr. Ricker chanced to come around the turret and discovered what I was doing and for about a minute the air was full of epithets which certainly were not complimentary to my wisdom and discretion. How many kinds of a fool he called me I cannot recall, and that he didn't order me put in irons in a coal bunker seems to me, even now, rather surprising.

I said nothing until Mr. Ricker's wrath had somewhat subsided, then I told him that the rope hung absolutely slack, and that there was nothing at all on the end which hung down in the water. "How do you *know* that?" he fiercely demanded, and I told him it "felt" slack, felt exactly like a fish-line with no sinker on the end of it!

Captain Cornwall had come on deck again by this time, and was interestedly listening to what we were saying. He now told Mr. Ricker that if I was quite sure there was nothing on the end of the line that I be ordered to draw the rope up out of the water, slowly, but to take care to keep the rope the length of the boat-hook away from the side of the ship.

Asking the man who had earlier held the keg away from the ship to hold the boat-hook in such a way that the rope would be drawn up over the Y-shaped end of it, I began to slowly draw up the rope. I confess that I felt decidedly like "funking"! I wished myself well out of the scrape before I had pulled up two yards of that line. But by the time I had drawn up a dozen feet of it, my confidence in the "slack feel" of it had returned and I was absolutely certain there was nothing weighty attached to the end of it. When about sixty feet of line lay on the deck behind me and the end came up out of the water, I saw that the end was a simple "bight", and I wanted to let out a shout, so great was my relief.

Taking the end of the rope directly to Mr. Ricker I called his attention to some particles of iron-rust on the inside of the bight, that iron-rust being pretty good proof that the bight had been attached by an iron ring to some anchoring device. The other officers gathered about to examine my prize, and while they were doing so I thought it a good time to disappear from the deck. I had no business to have been mixed up with the investigating of the floating object, and besides, I had had no breakfast!

During the forenoon the supposed torpedo was swung in over the deck and the wooden plug was pulled out of the fuse-plug base. Upon inverting the former beer keg over a leather cartridge-bucket, some fifty or sixty pounds of coarse black powder was emptied out of it. Then everybody felt relieved and many laughed. What possible harm could come to one of the ironclads from the explosion of fifty or sixty pounds of powder on the surface of the water alongside? There was five feet of solid oak timbers faced with four inches of iron plates between the hull of the ship and the point where the explosion would take place!

When the officers were afterwards discussing this supposed torpedo, it was suggested that it was the intention that the keg be drawn down under a monitor's overhang, should we attempt to force our way through the obstructions, and that the explosion would then be under the overhang and against the half-inch-thick hull. . . . In such case there was some possibility of a monitor's hull being somewhat damaged, but the chance of such a floating mine (for that is what it was) being drawn down under the overhang was decidedly remote. The shape of those vessels was such with the sides of the overhang perpendicular that a loosely-floating object would simply be pushed to one side if the vessel came in contact with it.

Everyone on board felt much relieved after we had dissected and fully discussed the supposed-to-be-dangerous "obstruction," which had escaped from its anchor and floated down to us that Sunday morning.

During these summer nights when the weather and our not being up on picket duty permitted of our sleeping on deck, we now enjoyed the spectacle of the mortar shells from Fort Moultrie and the batteries on Sullivan's Island climbing towards the sky, then circling over and down into or near to Fort Wagner. The tables were now turned, and the Confederate gunners were endeavoring to retard the repairs which the Union troops were making on their new possession.

There was little of interest for my diary to record during several weeks. Aside from the state of the weather, or the fact that we were "up on picket" or "coaling ship" or "the supply steamer *Massachusetts* came in," the chief entries are "Occasional firing from Fort Moultrie and the Confederate batteries."

On the night of October 5–6 a daring and partly successful attempt was made to sink the *Ironsides*. A new boat of unusual design had been built by a citizen of Charleston for the Confederate navy. It was shaped like a cigar, was about fifty feet in length and five and one-half feet in diameter in the centre, tapered to a point at each end, and when ready for duty was almost wholly submerged. At its bow was hinged a hollow iron shaft about fourteen feet long, which carried at the end a copper-cylinder torpedo which was charged with a hundred pounds of rifle powder and provided with four sensitive tubes of lead which contained an explosive mixture. A line from the torpedo passed over a pulley at the top of a short mast set upon the bow and thence to the captain who sat at the wheel just within the hatchway and gave to that officer control of the elevation of the torpedo. This boat was equipped with a compact steam engine and boiler and was operated by the captain and three men.

On the evening of October 5th this little "David", as it was called,[3] commanded by Lieutenant [William T.] Glassell of the Confederate Navy, made its way down the harbor soon after dark, and steamed outside the fleet of ironclads so as to be able to have the aid of the light from camp-fires on Morris Island in locating the vessels of the fleet. In due time the huge bulk of the *Ironsides* could be seen and her broadside was presented to attack. Putting on all steam, the "David" made for its victim, but it was discovered by the sentries on watch on the frigate's deck while it was still some distance away and hailed several times.

The officer of the deck had come to the gangway the better to observe the approaching object, and was plainly in view against the sky-line as the "David" drew near the frigate. Lieutenant Glassell reached down behind him for his gun and taking careful aim fired, mortally wounding the officer of the deck on the *Ironsides*. The next instant the torpedo came in contact with the hull of the frigate and exploded with great force.

Unfortunately for the torpedo-boat, most of the force of the explosion was expended upon the water, and a huge geyser-like eruption rose into the air, the bulk of it descending upon the deck of the frigate and much of it going down the engine-room hatch to the consternation of the officers and men on duty there who imagined for a few moments that their ship was going down. A considerable quantity

3. The original *David* was a "cigar-shaped" steam vessel, fifty feet long with a crew of four. It was this vessel that attacked the *New Ironsides* on the night of 5 October 1863. Encouraged by its near success, the Confederates built other similar vessels all of which came to be called "Davids" after the prototype, much as the *Monitor* gave its name to a whole class of vessels.

of the water fell back upon the "David", going down the open hatch-way in such quantity as to extinguish the fire, and the boat was disabled.

Realizing that his situation was desparate, Lieutenant Glassell ordered his men to abandon the boat, and with two of the men, he took to the water as his boat drifted astern of the frigate and floated away. After floating along for some time, Lieutenant Glassell was picked up by a coal schooner and made prisoner and one of his men was soon after discovered clinging to the rudder chains of the *Ironsides* and captured.

One of the four, unable to swim, did not leave the "David" but drifted along in it until he found one of his companions floating near. After assisting this man into the boat, they investigated matters and finally succeeded in getting a fire started under the boiler, raised sufficient steam to start the engine, and the two managed to guide the miniature craft back to Charleston.

On board the *Ironsides* there was great consternation for a time. The huge frigate was shaken from stem to stern by the force of the explosion, and the deluge which descended into the engine-room added to the panic-condition there. Taken by and large, it is not strange that the officers and men were apprehensive that the ship might have been seriously damaged, might even then be sinking!

Admiral Dahlgren was not on board the flagship at the time of the explosion, but quickly returned to it and although divers who were sent down to investigate reported that no material damage had been done, he recorded in his diary: "It seems to me nothing could have been more successful as a first effort, and it will place the *torpedo* among *certain* offensive means."

Captain Roman, commanding the *Ironsides*, the next day made report to the admiral as follows:

> Sir: I have the honor to report the circumstances attending the explosion of a torpedo against the side of this ship last night at a quarter past nine o'clock;
> About a minute before the explosion a small object was seen by the sentinels and hailed by them as a boat, and also by Mr. Howard, officer of the deck, from the gangway. Receiving no answer, he gave the order "Fire into her." The sentinels delivered their fire, and immediately the ship received a very severe blow from the explosion, throwing a column of water upon the spar deck and into the engine room. The object fired at proved to be

(as I subsequently learned from one of the prisoners) a torpedo steamer, shaped like a cigar, 50 feet long by five feet in diameter, and of great speed, and so submerged, that the only portion of her visible was the coamings of her hatch, which were only 2 feet above the water's edge and about 10 feet in length.

The torpedo-boat was commanded by Lieutenant Commanding Glassell, formerly a lieutenant in our Navy and now our prisoner. He states that the explosion threw a column of water over the little craft, which put out the fires and left it without motive power, and it drifted past the ship.

Nothing could be seen from the gundeck, and to fire at random would endanger the fleet of transports and other vessels near us. The marine guard and musketeers on the spar deck saw a small object at which a very severe fire was kept up until it drifted out of sight, when two of the monitors, the *Weehawken* and *Catskill*, passed under our stern and were close to it, when it suddenly disappeared. Two of our cutters were despatched in search of it, but returned without success.

I hope our fire destroyed the torpedo-steamer, and infer the fact from the statement of Lieutenant Commanding Glassell, who acknowledges that he and engineer Tomb and pilot, who constituted the crew at the time of the explosion, were compelled to abandon the vessel, and being provided with life-preservers, swam for their lives. Glassell hailed one of our coal-schooners as he drifted past, and was rescued from a grave he designed for the crew of this ship.[4]

That this torpedo attack upon the *Ironsides* was only partially successful seems to have been due to the fact that the torpedo struck the side of that vessel at a depth of three or four feet below the surface of the water where there was three inches thickness of iron armor. Thus there was . . . greater resistance of iron armor, plus the great weight of the ship, than of water above—hence the "geyser" which went up into the air and so nearly swamped the torpedo-boat.

Had the torpedo been lowered into the water to a depth of, say, ten or twelve feet, it would have been exploded against the hull of the ship and the force of the explosion would have been supported by the great weight of water above it. In that case the frigate would doubtless have gone down in a very few minutes, and torpedo warfare would have taken on a great impetus. Speculation as to what might have been is rather profitless, but it is probable that Lieutenant Glassell would

4. Rowan to Dahlgren, 6 October 1863. ORN, I, 15:12–13.

have had time to duly lower the torpedo-arm had he not been tempted to take a shot at Officer-of-the-deck Howard on the *Ironsides*. He shot and mortally wounded the officer, but failed to lower the torpedo-arm and so failed to sink his foe!

Accounts of the injury to the *Ironsides* by the torpedo differ greatly, some wildly exaggerated statements made by Confederates being to the effect that she was so much disabled as never to have fired another shot. These statements are wholly disproved by the fact that the *Ironsides* remained on duty there in the outer harbor of Charleston for several months, and then led the ironclad division in the attacks upon Fort Fisher, North Carolina, in December 1864 and January 1865. She was in action some forty hours in all during those two battles.

Admiral Dahlgren, in his "Memoir", states: "Nov. 18. Captain Rowan came on board to report that, in removing coal in bunkers of *Ironsides*, it was discovered that the injury from torpedo was very serious, and extended down toward the keel."[5]

Dr. Scharf, in his *History of the Confederate States Navy*, states that:

> Upon examining the *New Ironsides*, it was found that the torpedo exploded only three feet under water and against 4½ inches of armor, and 27 inches of wood backing. By the explosion the ponderous ship was shaken from stem to stern. It knocked down a bulkhead, started some timbers, and threw two or three rooms into confusion. A marine was dashed against a ceiling and his leg broken, while several other men were slightly injured.[6]

Mr. J. Vaughan Merrick of Philadelphia, builder of the *Ironsides*, in a paper contributed to the "Journal of the Franklin Institute" of that city, stated that "beyond driving a deck-beam on end and shattering a knee no material damage was done to the ship." This paper is also quoted as authority for the statement that: "the armor of the *Ironsides*, for a distance of four feet below the load-line, was three inches thick." *Not* four and a half inches, as stated by Dr. Scharf.[7]

---

5. Madeleine V. Dahlgren, *Memoir of John A. Dahlgren* (New York, 1891), 426.
6. J. Thomas Scharf, *History of the Confederate States Navy from its Organization to the Surrender of the Last Vessel* (New York, 1887), 760.
7. In fact, the 4.5-inch armor belt on the *New Ironsides* covered only about 170 of the 230 feet of the hull. The bow and stern were largely unarmored. The *David's* torpedo exploded against the ship's unarmored quarter.

It is certain that the moral effect of this torpedo-attack was very great. To the end of the war there was a lively apprehension of further attacks, and a most elaborate system of protection was put in operation at once. Many picket-boats were put on guard every night, and two tugs were kept slowly moving about the frigate while a revolving calcium light sent its rays over the water in every direction. Fenders, similar to those with which the monitors had protected themselves in the North Edisto after the threatened torpedo-attack in the spring, were now stretched at twenty-feet distance from the sides of all the ironclads, and the utmost viligance was maintained at night.

15 | A Day's Liberty

Visiting Fort Wagner and Battery Gregg

FOR OVER A WEEK FOLLOWING THE TORPEDO ATTACK UPON THE *Ironsides*, the *Nahant* was up-channel on picket duty every night, and we were coaling ship during the last three days of the week ending October 17. Picket duty nights and coaling ships during the days was decidedly strenuous work for the crew, but the men quickly forgot their fatigue when word was passed that on Sunday half of them would be given a day's liberty on shore, and that the other half would be given liberty on the following Sunday.

It had not been the custom to give the wardroom boys liberty with the men chiefly because we had so much more freedom in going about in the dinghy it was thought unnecessary to give us special liberty days. Now, however, as visiting about with the dinghy had been cut off for several weeks, one wardroom boy was to be given the day. Both Barney and George had been in durance [imprisoned] recently so they were passed, and my record being quite clean I was told that if I cared to have the day on shore with the men I could do so.

Sunday morning the liberty men togged themselves out in their best, and most of them certainly dressed for the occasion. Boatswain's mate Vincent, in silk socks and patent-leather pumps (the latter ornamented with small bows of black-silk ribbon) led the file of men both literally and in the matter of dress. [He] stood at the gangway overseeing the stowing of the men in the 2d cutter and on board a life-raft which was pressed into service for the occasion.

This life-raft was a recent acquisition and was familiarly called

"The Catamaran". It consisted of four huge tubes of stout rubber secured to the underside of a light frame-work of wood on which there were four oarlocks. When the rubber tubes were inflated, they were about eighteen inches in diameter and very buoyant. The raft was eight feet long by six feet wide, and even with eight or ten men on board it bobbed about like a cork. Similar life-rafts with buoying tubes made of metal instead of rubber, are now [1924] to be seen on the spar-decks of all passenger-carrying steamships.

There were about thirty of us "liberty men", eight or ten on the life raft which was towed behind the cutter, and four non-liberty men went along to row the cutter and raft back to the ship. The great advantage of having the life-raft along was manifest when we approached the shore of Morris Island. The water is very shallow for some distance out, and heavily loaded boat could not come nearer than two hundred feet of the beach. The life-raft, however, could float close in to the beach and then a running jump would usually land one above the slight surf. Now and then one of the men would wet his feet and it pleased me to see Vincent's silk socks and patent-leather pumps get well soaked as he plumped them into the surf. But nobody minded a little thing like that—it was "Liberty Day"!

All up and down the beach soldiers were fishing, and having been an ardent fisherman from the time I was four and a half years old, I at once turned to watch the fishing operations. All of the fishermen were barefooted, hence prepared to wade into the water a bit when there was advantage in so doing. They were fishing with hand-lines a hundred to a hundred and fifty feet long which they adroitly coiled up in the left hand as they drew the line slowly in, then they tossed it far out again by giving with the right hand a couple of swings to the hook and three or four feet of line, and letting the hook sail out over the water, drawing after it the line released from the left hand coils. Many of these fishermen were very expert in throwing out their hooks and as a rule it seemed to be the ones who got their hooks farthest out that caught the biggest fish.

As I strolled along the beach I recognized a sergeant of a Maine regiment whose acquaintance I had made at Hilton Head and after a few minutes' chat with him I asked what steps I would have to take to obtain permission to visit Fort Wagner, provided permission was necessary. He told me he wasn't certain as to either point, but he thought permission would be necessary and that I could obtain a pass from the

Provost Marshal, who had his office in a tent above which a flag was flying near the summit of one of the nearer sand-hills.

Thanking the sergeant I started on down the beach, stopping two or three times to watch the operation of pulling a fish ashore. When I had walked for a little way I decided to go inland and get into the camps, but had barely left the shore when I met two officers and asked them about a pass to visit Fort Wagner, telling them what the sergeant had said and adding that he hadn't felt sure. They were not certain that I could obtain a permit to visit Wagner, "but the Provost Marshall can give you a permit if anyone can, and you'll find his office up by that flag", pointing to a flag floating from a flagstaff on a hill a quarter-mile away.

Walking through the loose sand wasn't easy, but in due time I approached the tent above which the flag was flying and was trapped by a sentry who was marching up and down before it. Learning that I wished an interview with the Provost Marshall he bade me wait, walked to the entrance to the tent, saluted and spoke to the officer, then turned and said: "You may go in." I stopped in the entrance to the tent and saluted and was greeted with a smile. Doubtless the sight of a diminutive figure in a sailor's uniform surmounted by a decidedly boyish face *was* unusual, and the officer's amusement was warranted.

I stated my errand, and his face at once became "official." "And what my be your object in visiting Fort Wagner?" he asked. I told him that the *Nahant* had some pretty hard knocks from Wagner, and now that I had a day's liberty ashore I very much wished to visit that fort but solely from curiosity. He asked me several questions, his purpose probably being to detect whether I was as honest as I pretended to be, and finally he said: "Well, it is within my authority to give you a pass to Wagner, but it is most unusual, most unusual!" He had repeated the last words in a musing way as though he was considering whether he oughtn't to refuse my request. I told him, frankly, that I very much desire to visit Fort Wagner and Battery Gregg, and that a boy such as I was couldn't do any harm there, and that I would endeavor to keep out of the way, etc. etc.

After a little reflection he said: "Well, I'm going to give you the pass, but you will be running some risk up there. The rebels are shelling Wagner every day, and you might get your foolish head shot off, you know!" I told him I'd take all the risk and thanked him for the concession. He drew a stub-book of blank passes to him and asked my name. After he had filled out and signed the pass, he read it over [then] looked up and said: "I suppose you'll want to return as well as go up there, won't you?" I acknowledged that such was my expectation, and he laughed as he said: "I'll just write '& return' on it, so if you don't meet with any mishap you will have no difficulty in leaving." Again thanking Mr. Provost Marshall I saluted, pocketed the pass, and walked out.

Having secured my pass there was no need to hurry, so I went to the top of a nearby sand-hill to get a view of the fleet on the water and the camps on the island, then turned down toward the camps to see how the soldiers lived and how they were enjoying the day. As I was walking along a regimental street, I noticed some commotion just ahead and when I came nearer saw a dozen or fifteen men gathered about one of their number who had secured a canteen of liquor and was selling "nips" of it to his comrades.

One of the men saw me and called out: "Here's a 'Jacky' from the fleet, give him a nip." I replied: "Thank you, but I never drink liquor!" and turned to go on my way. The man ran after me and exclaimed: "What t'ell do yer mean! *Every* Jacky drinks liquor! Come on now, have one on me, mate." He was decidedly rough in manner and I had visions of trouble, but two or three of the others had come up by this time and one of them said: "Oh! Let 'im alone, Bill, he's only a kid! If he don't *want* a drink don't yer make 'im drink, and there's a nip more for you or me, See?" Probably the last part of the argument was the more potent; at any rate I thought it a good time to leave, and left.

Making my way down to the shore, where the sand was harder and the walking easier, I started north. There were so many men fishing, however, my progress up the shore was frequently halted by some interesting sight, and it was high noon when I approached Wagner and looked about for the way into it.

There was a short row of piles extending down towards the water from the corner of the fort, and a sentry appeared just beyond this barricade. He halted upon seeing me and I walked up to him and presented my pass. He looked at it, then called out: "Corporal of the Guard." In a few seconds the head of that official appeared above the parapet. He paused for a moment to give me a look-over, then came down a slanting path which brought him to the beach. The sentry handed him my pass, which he read and then said: "That's all right, come on up," and I followed him up the path to the top of the parapet.

Fort Wagner lay spread out before me like a map, and I stood for some minutes gazing at the many interesting objects. Some fatigue parties were at work with wheelbarrows and shovels removing sand from the interior of the fort and wheeling it up an incline to the parapet from which it had been "shoveled" by General Gillmore's shots, and there were, I would guess, two hundred men scattered over the different sections of the work. In answer to my remark that the wheelbarrow and shovel men didn't seem to be very enthusiastic over their work, the corporal told me that they were only working as a punishment for some petty breaches of discipline and that the regular repair work was omitted on Sundays.

Leading the way down to the guardroom he handed my pass to the sergeant in command with the remark: "That seems to be all right." The sergeant nodded in reply as he handed the pass back to me and asked: "Had any dinner?" I told him that I had brought two or three sandwiches with me and that if I could beg a drink of water I'd sit there and eat with them, for they were eating their dinner. A canteen of water was handed me, with the invitation to make myself at home, and we chatted sociably as we ate. The sergeant told me that it was decidedly unusual for a sailor from the fleet to come a way up there: "In fact," he said, "You're the first one that *I've* seen up here. There were a couple of officers from the flagship came up with our captain one day last week, but you're the first sailorman that I've seen up here!" I told him that I wasn't seventeen yet, and probably wasn't much of a sailorman, anyway. We talked about the hard hits Fort Wagner had given the monitors, and both the sergeant and corporal seemed interested in what I could tell them. They were especially interested in my story of our experience under Sumter in April. Thanking them for their hospitality, I told them I'd look about for a while then intended to go up to Battery Gregg.

Fort Wagner had originally been built as a battery and it stood near the spot from whence the first hostile shot of the Civil War was fired. This was a shot fired at the steamer *Star of the West* which was on its way to Fort Sumter with food and supplies for Major Anderson and his men. The *Star of the West* was turned back, and Fort Sumter failed to receive the needed supplies.[1]

1. The *Star of the West* was an unarmed merchant steamer sent by the Buchanan administration to re-supply Fort Sumter in January 1861. As it approached Charleston Harbor on the mornings of 9 January, the Confederates opened fire from the Morris Island batteries. Technically, these were the first shots fired in the Civil War.

When Battery Wagner was enlarged and became the strong earth-work which we knew as Fort Wagner, it was built (roughly stated) in the shape of the letter "L", with the base of the letter the sea-face, which extended north along the beach some two hundred and fifty or three hundred feet, and the shank of the letter was the south-face, looking down the island, and extended west across the "neck" of the island at this narrow place. Vincent's Creek makes a deep curve into Morris Island from the inner harbor, and at this point there was but seven or eight hundred feet of island between the creek and the beach. The south-face of Wagner occupied all of this space.

On the north and west the fort was enclosed by modest parapets, made available for infantry to repel a possible assault upon these sides, and there were perhaps half a dozen field pieces mounted there. All of the heavy guns were mounted upon the south and sea-faces of the fort, and some of them were so mounted, in bastions, that they could be used in defense of either face of the fort in case an enemy was assaulting that face.

Fort Wagner certainly was a powerful earth-work; an hour spent in studying its position and lay-out would satisfy anyone that there was good reason why it had so effectively resisted the heavy attacks made upon it. General Gillmore, in his report to the general-in-chief in Washington in which he reports that the Confederates had been driven from it and that it was now in possession of his men, said:

> Fort Wagner is a work of the most formidable kind. Its bombproof shelter, capable of holding 1,800 men, remains intact after the most terrible bombardment to which any work was ever subjected. We have captured nineteen pieces of artillery and a large supply of excellent amunition.[2]

The bombproofs were nearest, and I turned into one of them with a live curiosity to find just inside the door three or four sets of card players indulging in the favorite game of "seven-up," and scattered about on the sand-floor were dozens of men asleep. There were two or three large apartments underneath the ramparts, and they looked to be very comfortable retreats from the heat of the sun or the danger of an enemy's shells. My recollection of the spaciousness of those bomb-proofs does not quite "square" with the statement in Johnson's *Defence of Charleston Harbor*, which says, in the report of conditions within

2. Gillmore to Halleck, 7 September 1863. ORA, I, 28:206.

the fort during the fierce bombardment of September 5 & 6, that "hardly one-half [of the 900 men] could have endured the heat and crowding of those close quarters."[3] Perhaps General Gillmore's statement that there was room there for 1,800 men errs in the other direction, but I feel sure that the 900 men of the Confederate garrison would have been less uncomfortable in those good-sized bombproofs than they were in the nearly shelterless sand-knolls to the north of the fort of which Captain Johnson tells us.

Ascending to the south-east bastion, I had a good look at the banded-rifled gun there, one of the two heavy guns which had given the *Nahant* the hardest knocks. It was, indeed, a formidable-looking gun, but during the last days of our experiences with Wagner, it had been less active than the X-inch columbiad until the latter had been dismounted by the lucky shot from the *Ironsides.* It was my guess that there was a scarcity of amunition for this rifled gun, that facilities for making the peculiar "bolts" used in his Brooke, Whitworth, and Parrott rifled guns were somewhat lacking in the Confederate States.[4]

A youthful-looking lieutenant came up into the bastion while I was enjoying the view over the harbor towards Charleston. We chatted a bit over our two branches of the service, and were suddenly interrupted by a call from a sentry who was walking a beat on the west parapet, who called out: "Cover-r-r Johnson-n-n!" and I turned my eyes westward towards Fort Johnson in time to see the smoke of the gun and a shot coming in our direction. Then we heard the boom of the gun and scream of a rifled shot. A "chuck" from the marsh over near Vincent's Creek told that the shot had fallen short of Wagner, and the lieutenant exclaimed: "What a lot of amunition those fools are wasting!" "Do they usually miss the mark?" I asked. "Oh, yes," he replied. "They miss us nine times out of ten! And when they do hit the fort they do no damage," he continued. "You see how little the men care for the shots, not one hunted cover." This was quite true. Not a man, so far as I could see, had paid any attention to the sentry's warning call.

I asked the lieutenant about the X-inch columbiad which had been dismounted, and he led the way along the parapet of the sea-face to the low mound of sand which had so long protected that gun from the

3. Johnson, 149.
4. By 1863 the Confederacy was short of all types of specialized ammunition and unable to manufacture or import all it needed.

shots of the fleet. At the foot of the mound, at the rear, stood the disabled gun, looking somewhat like a monument so upright was it, and the trunnion missing from one side made it suggetive of a pet seal I had once seen that had a trick of folding down one of his flippers which gave him a decidedly ludicrous appearance. Only the seal would need to be standing on his head, for the gun had landed on its breach when it was thrown back and downward by the dismounting shot, and it stood just where it had landed, almost upright, with a slight incline towards the north-east.

Study of the method of mounting that gun greatly increased my admiration for the man who had planned it out. Just a few feet south of the north bastion, a mound of sand had been erected and a gently inclining platform had been put down on which the recoil of the gun carried it back and down behind the sand-mound, and when a shot discharged as the gun reached the parapet where the muzzle of the gun had been, the gun itself was safely resting behind twenty-feet-thickness of protecting sand. Just how the quarter-curve of the platform (or track) had been taken by the trucks of the gun-carriage could not be seen as the carriage had been destroyed by fire and the track itself had been removed, possibly to provide fuel for the soldiers' camp fires. This was certainly an ingenious way to have a gun disappear from view the instant it was discharged. So far as I know this was the earliest example of "disappearing guns".

Realizing that my time was slipping away, I thanked the lieutenant for his courtesy and started up the shore towards Battery Gregg from which a shot was now and then being fired at Fort Sumter. Battery Gregg was a modest little fortification mounting three guns about three-fourths of a mile distant from Sumter, and from the top of its parapet I had a fine view of Fort Moultrie and the batteries of Sullivan's Island. Also I could clearly see the row of obstructions stretching across the channel beyond Sumter. The latter looked to be but a tumbled down heap of bricks and mortar on that side, but a small Confederate flag was floating from a short staff set up on the angle of the gorge and east-face, which told that the garrison was alert.

A sergeant seemed to be in command of the firing squad at the gun nearest Sumter, and to him I handed my pass. He glanced at it and called my attention to a lieutenant who was reading a book as he sat in the shade of one of the other gun-carriages. Going over to him I was greeted with: "Hello, Jack! What brought you away up here?" I told him I was ashore "on liberty", and was taking liberties. He laughed heartily, glanced at my pass, and as he handed it back he asked if there was anything he could do for me. I told him I just wanted to have a look-around and wanted to see the sergeant fire a shot or two at Sumter then must return to the boat as the day was going fast. He said the gun would be fired again in a minute or two. I saluted and returned to the side of the sergeant.

The gun was being pointed as I reached its vicinity and when ready the sergeant pulled the lanyard, then stepped onto the gun-carriage with his field glasses at his eyes to watch the effect of the shot. I could easily follow it with the naked eye, saw it go sailing through the air towards the broad target, and a small cloud of dust arose from the place where it struck in the heap of rubbish. It had been aimed at the flagstaff and struck just a bit west of and below it. "Too much allowance for the wind," said the sergeant, and then he sat down to await the next loading of the gun. In answer to my questions, he told me they were firing three or four times an hour, and were firing those shots because there was considerable amunition in the magazine which had been left when the Confederates evacuated the island and it was thought best to use it. "We are not doing any great amount of damage," he said, "but we are letting them know we are not asleep."

I asked the loan of the field glasses and was told they belonged to the officer. The sergeant glanced over at him, and seeing that he was absorbed in his book, handed me the glasses with a gesture of the other hand which I understood to mean "go ahead," and I mounted the parapet to get a good view of Sumter, the fortifications on Sullivan's Island, and the city. This look-around I greatly appreciated.

I waited to see another shot fired at Sumter, then bade the sergeant good day and started back, saluting the lieutenant as he glanced up from his book as I was passing. He acknowledged the salute and smiled at me and I headed for Wagner again. I made directly for it along a beaten path which was more direct than the curving shore, entering the fort by the north-east bastion so as to get another good look at our old friend—the dismounted X-inch Columbiad. That gun was certainly the most pleasing sight of the day, as it stood erect there in the position in which it had landed. The ending of that gun's activities was a most efficient piece of work.

I passed my hand over the place where the trunnion had been and found there was a slight depression in the metal, which showed that the break was not quite as even as it at first glance appeared to be. There were signs that there had been fire close by the gun, and in Johnson's

Defence I find the following, quoted from the journal of a captain Huguenin who was chief of artillery in Wagner just before the evacuation:

> Soon after daylight the cry of 'Fire!' startled me, and, hurrying out, I found that just in the gun-pit next our principal magazine the carriage of a 10-inch columbiad, which had been struck the day before, was in flames. The gun was standing up almost perpendicular, the trunion having been broken off; and I knew that as soon as the piece became heated it would be discharged and thrown violently backward, to the injury of our only remaining magazine. So without water to put out the fire, what was to be done? Seizing a shovel, I called aloud to some men near by to assist me in throwing sand upon the fire. We checked it, and then, procuring a kettle of water, we poured its contents down the muzzle and destroyed the powder of the charge. This was a narrow escape, and, knowing the importance of it, I worked so hard that I nearly fainted.[5]

I crossed the parade to the west-face of the fort and watched Fort Johnson for a few minutes, hoping there would be another shot fired at Wagner while I stood there, then walked over to and along the south-face of the fort to the south-east bastion where was our other old friend, the banded-rifled gun. Here I said my "good bye" to Fort Wagner, walked down to the guardroom and handed my pass to the corporal. He walked over the parapet with me and down to the row of piles. I thanked him again for his kindness and he held out his hand to me, we smiled our good byes, and I hastened down the shore for I had noted that the cutter had put off from the *Nahant* just as I left the south-east bastion of Wagner.

I had gone not more than a dozen steps from where I had left the corporal when the warning cry, "Cover-r-r Johnson-n-n!" again rang out. I stopped and looked west, towards the fort on the tip of James Island, saw the smoke of the gun and saw the shot rising and coming straight towards me! I was certain that shot would strike just where I stood, but for the life of me, I couldn't move my feet from the spot! In a few seconds I saw the shot strike eighty or a hundred feet west of where I was standing, then it went tumbling end over end on into the water. It passed fifteen or twenty feet south of where I stood and if I had kept on walking I would have been very-very close to the place

---

5. Johnson, Appendix, cxiii.

where it went tumbling across the beach. Needless to state, the "roar" of that rifle shot hastened my footsteps down the shore.

[When I] arrived at the place where we had come ashore, I found some of my mates already there, and part of them were a decidedly sorry-looking lot. Nearly all of them were the worse for liquor. Some had evidently been fighting, and one poor chap had a most distressing-looking nose and black eye. Others came down to the shore in the same sorry condition, some of them being helped along by their less-intoxicated mates, and all looked a very different lot of men from the happy group that had come ashore a few hours before.

The cutter was anchored a hundred feet or more out from the beach and the life-raft took us off to the boat a half-dozen at a time. Not all got down to the shore in season to be taken back to the ship that night. Five or six of the men had to be hunted up and brought aboard in irons the next day.

And this was the end of "A Day's Liberty!"

16 ‖ THREE WEEKS IN PORT ROYAL

NEAR TO A DISASTER

THE *LEHIGH* AGROUND

FOR SEVERAL WEEKS ONE OR ANOTHER OF THE MONITORS HAD BEEN sent in turn to Port Royal to refit and to give the men a respite from their exacting duties, usually one monitor returning to the fleet on one day and another going off the next. On the 19th of October the *Patapsco* rejoined the fleet and the next afternoon the *Nahant* left for Port Royal, arriving at that restful haven on the morning of the 21st. Mention has been made of the efforts to rid the ship's hull of the barnacles and other marine growth, and much time was now given to completing that important work.

The next morning after our arrival at Port Royal, the *Nahant* steamed up into shallow water a little way west of the naval machine-shop, and gently floated inshore till she touched on the soft bottom. It was then just before the beginning of the ebb tide, and in half an hour the ship was quietly resting on the mud-bottom. Two long floats, each made by lashing three discarded spars together and then a deck of old planks nailed down on them, were towed alongside. When the tide had receded so that the hull began to be exposed, the men went onto the floats and scraped away at the barnacles. It was great fun for the men: The water was still fairly warm, the men were dressed in their oldest and most-worn clothes, and an hour had not passed before most of them were off the floats and in the water up to or above the middle, making a genuine "sailors' lark" of the scraping.

As the tide receded more, they could reach farther down under the hull, and when it was near low water, half a dozen buckets of red paint were passed down, with a couple of paint brushes to each bucket, and part of the men went to painting the part of the hull where the barnacles has been scraped off, or as far down as they could reach without going under water. There was but about half an hour of dead low water, and they had to work fast at the painting while the water was low, and as the tide rose the men drew back from under the hull, painting as far as they could reach, and by the time the in-flowing tide had driven the men back to the floats one side of the hull was pretty well cleaned and painted; the work on that side was finished two or three days later.

The next day the port side of the hull was gone over in the same manner, and when the *Nahant* was pulled off the mud flats at high tide on the 24th, it was found that she could move through the water under her own steam much faster than for some time previous. Notwithstanding all that had been done, the officers felt that there were portions of the hull, especially far aft, that were not thoroughly clean, so we steamed back onto the mud-flat again at high tide on the 26th, and more scraping and painting was done as the state of the water favored.

On Sunday, October 25th, the men who had not had "liberty" on the previous Sunday were given the day, and they spent it ashore at Hilton Head. When they returned aboard late in the afternoon the drunkenness and disorder of the week before was repeated. One scene of that coming aboard was very painful. A youthful sailor named Horatio Young, a handsome fellow and generally liked, was completely paralyzed in the lower limbs by the liquor he had taken aboard. He was lifted out of the boat by his mates, propelled himself across the deck by pawing with his arms and hands, and when he reached the berth deck hatch he just let himself go and rolled down the companionway to the deck below. Three weeks later this man was promoted on the spot by Admiral Dahlgren for gallantry in action, as told in the latter part of this chapter.

October 27th was my birthday; the only entry in my diary for that day simply tells: "Seventeen years old today."

During the first week at Port Royal we boys had resumed our pleasure trips in the dinghy, although most of the trips were made in the line of duty, such, for example, as transporting four or five bags of wash-clothes to a cabin near the shore at Bay Point and several days later going ashore after them; and on two different days rowing the caterer for the wardroom mess to Hilton Head to purchase table supplies at the stores there. On both days that we went to Bay Point we had our usual swimming frolic, and enjoyed the swims all the more because we knew the season was about over. Boy-like, however, we made the most of it while it lasted.

October 31st the *Nahant* steamed alongside the old frigate *Vermont*, which had a huge black cylinder suspended by a tackle from her main yard, and when we were warped into the exact position and made fast, the cylinder was slowly lowered into place, surrounding the pilot-house. The cylinder was called a "sleeve," and added two inches thickness to the defense strength of the pilot-house, which had been found rather weak for its greatly exposed position. The pilot-houses of the monitors were quite small, and it had been calculated that they were little likely to be struck fairly by heavy shot. They were, however, set just above the turrets, and as the turrets were the only prominent targets at which to point guns, quite a good many shots struck the pilot-houses, and they had been severely handled. This addition to their protective armor decidedly strengthened them.

On November 1st Lieutenant Thomas came on board and reported for duty, relieving Mr. Carter, who was 1st watch-officer and since Mr. Harmony left us had also been Executive Officer, or "second in command". The next day Mr. Carter sailed for the North, where he had been ordered to duty. On this day (November 2d), I received a small box of "goodies" from Aunt Hatch in Chelsea, and we boys had a feast of good things in addition to our regular fare. The box had been brought down by Mr. Clark, formerly one of our watch officers and now in command of a trading schooner loaded with supplies to sell to vessels of the fleet.

Powder, shot and shell were daily being taken aboard and stowed in the magazine and in vacant spaces below the berthdeck and wardroom floor. On the 6th and 7th we were coaling ship, and there was every indication that our holiday was over. On Sunday, November 8th, a new surgeon, Dr. Ricketts, came on board and reported for duty, and Dr. Stedman went north on sick leave. The departure of Mr. Carter and Dr. Stedman left us but two of our original officers on duty.

As a violent storm was raging on the 9th, we steamed down to the vicinity of the old *Vermont*, anchored there and waited. The next day there was a very heavy sea running outside and we continued to wait for better weather. On the 11th the conditions were satisfactory and we put out to sea. Ten or a dozen steamers and schooners that had been weatherbound for two or three days sailed from Port Royal that morning, and it was a gay sight as the fleet rounded the lightship and headed north. For the first time the *Nahant* was making a voyage under her own steam, was at sea without being towed.

There was a heavy swell outside, we had full stores of coal and ammunition on board, and the ship labored badly. We had not gone many miles from the lightship when it was reported to the officer of the deck that considerable water had found its way into the chain lockers beneath the windlass-room floor, and evidently wasn't flowing aft as it was expected to do, hence the pumps, which were all aft in the engine room, could not get at the water to pump it out. The hawse-hole, through which the anchor chain passed forward to the anchor well, had been caulked as tightly as possible, but still some water leaked in and accumulated in the chain lockers. After studying the matter for a little time and consulting the Chief Engineer, Captain Cornwall ordered that we turn about and return to Port Royal; we came to anchor near the *Vermont* about noon.

Several boats were soon alongside to make inquiry as to our turning back and ask if we needed assistance, and the Captain of the Port (the senior captain present) instructed Captain Cornwall to steam alongside a brig that was anchored near, and take advantage of a hoisting tackle on her main yard to hoist the shot and shell from our hold to the deck. This was done, and all the afternoon was spent in getting up and moving aft the heavy shot and shells that were weighing down the forward end of the ship. By evening the water began to find its way aft where the pumps could get to work upon it, and the considerable quantity which had accumulated forward gradually disappeared.

A "gradual disappearance," however, wasn't satisfactory. There was an open channel along each side of the keel, with holes cut through the braces of the frame so as to give free passage aft to any water which should make its way into the forward parts of the ship. When the coal bunkers were full and the forward end of the ship not overloaded, there was about a foot of downward slope from the bow back to the engine-room. With these drainage channels clear there should never be any water standing under the floor of the windlass room.

The stowage lockers beneath the wardroom and berthdeck were opened and all stores lifted out of them so as to lay bare the "skin" of the ship along the keel, and the men then thoroughly cleaned out the drainage channels clear aft to the engine room. Several of the openings through the braces were found clogged with chips and shavings which had been carelessly dropped into the hold by the carpenters laying the decks and fitting the hatches opening into the lockers. And back under the tureet chamber one of the openings was found to be neatly dammed by a wad of discarded cotton waste which had probably been carelessly dropped by one of the mechanics at work upon the machinery in the turret chamber. How astonished such workmen would be if told their carelessness had seriously jeopardized the safety of the vessel they had been at work upon!

That the *Nahant* had been in imminent danger of foundering there is no possible doubt. Had she continued on her course that day the water would have kept on accumulating in the chain-lockers forward until the always delicate balance of the hull was upset, then a dip into one of the heavy swells that were rolling in from the broad Atlantic and the *Nahant* would have gone to the bottom in exactly the same manner the *Weehawken* sank about four weeks later.[1] The intelligent foresight of the *Nahant's* officers had saved her from disaster, just as the intelligent foresight of one of the gunners had saved her from shooting down her own smokestack on June 17th, when the ram *Atlanta* was coming down upon us. Certainly the *Nahant* had been fortunate!

The work of cleaning out the bilge was completed soon after noon of November 12th. The stores and ammunition were again stowed in the lockers, but quite a number of solid shot were lowered into the engine-room and stowed there, so the afterpart of the ship would be in proper balance, and about three o'clock in the afternoon, we again passed the lightship off the bar and headed north. At two o'clock in the morning of the 13th, we dropped anchor off Charleston bar, and about eight o'clock in the morning we steamed in and came to anchor near the *Ironsides.*

Many things about the outer harbor of Charleston looked just as when the *Nahant* had left for Port Royal three weeks before, but Fort Sumter was "decidedly the worse for wear." A second great bombardment of Sumter had been begun October 26th by both the land batteries and ironclads, and the walls of that one-time formidable fortress appeared to be completely wrecked. The "angles" of the several faces of Sumter retained their shape and positions fairly well, but the face-walls were now little more than shapeless heaps of rubbish. Of this second great bombardment of Sumter Johnson's *Defense* says:

1. See Chapter Seventeen.

To describe the progress of this bombardment in as much detail as the first would not be a profitable task. The damages were less observable and the aggregate results less important. Yet its duration was more than twice as long as the other, and it differed widely in character from the former, being at close range for the rifle-guns and easy range for mortars, which were now for the first time employed by the enemy. In fact, these mortars seemed to predominate in the firing. Another prominent difference also was the constancy and vigor of the night-shelling.

But the leading events of the period are well worthy to be reviewed. The heaviest firing occurred in the first week or ten days of the bombardment. On two of these days more than one thousand projectiles per diem were discharged at the fort. The gorge and the sea-face appeared to be the parts aimed at by the rifles, and they soon began to show the effects of the fire. Its destructiveness was increased by the cross-firing of the monitors, two of them being under orders every day to cooperate with the land-batteries. They would take their station off the eastern or sea-face, and while the land-batteries were forced to deliver only a slant fire on the fort, they would throw against it, squarely, heavy rifle as well as smoothbore projectiles. In consequence, the ramparts and arches of the upper casemates were soon cut down and the debris, falling outside, formed now, for the first time, a practicable slope for assaulting-parties landing from small boats on this sea-face as well as on the gorge; while the ruins of the barracks, accumulating on the inside, gave the garrison in some places an easy ramp for ascending to the crest of the wall. The two angles, however, at the respective extremities of the sea-face, maintained their original height, lessened only by the destruction of the parapet. The crest of the gorge, though not reduced in height, except at one place, was much worn away and sharpened. A remark occurring in the *Diary* of the rear-admiral at this date is highly descriptive: "The heaps of rubbish at the gorge looks invincible."[2]

The *Nahant* at once went on duty with the ironclads. We were up-channel on picket duty on the nights of November 14th and 15th, and on the latter night the *Lehigh* was our companion. The forts and batteries on Sullivan's and James Islands kept up a pretty constant fire upon the Union troops on Morris Island, and my diary mentions that on the night of the 15th this fire of the Confederate batteries was very

2. Johnson, 170–71.

sharp. On the morning of the 16th we hoisted anchor soon after daybreak and steamed down to the anchorage of the fleet. The *Lehigh* did not get underway at the same time, but as this occasionally happened we thought nothing of it until, just as we were about to anchor, half a dozen signal flags broke out from her signal flagstaff and almost at the same moment Fort Moultrie opened fire upon her. The *Lehigh* was aground on one of the numerous shoals, and was in a far more dangerous situation than had been the *Weehawken* when she had been aground a few weeks previous, because she was much nearer the heavy guns of Fort Moultrie.

The *Nahant's* engine not having stopped, she at once turned about and steamed back up-channel, soon followed by the other monitors. Our galley smokepipe had been put up when we started down to the anchorage and the cooks had got the galley fire going; the smokepipe was quickly taken down again, but the fire in the galley wasn't so easily disposed of. The hot coal was shoveled out into an iron bucket and toted back to the fireroom where it was fed to the furnaces, but much coal-gas had escaped while this was being done, and life on the berthdeck was most uncomfortable for a half-hour or more, but we were so busy, little attention was paid to the extra discomfort. Before we had come up near to the *Lehigh* our guns were at work, and no more strenuous firing was ever done by any two-gun monitor than we did in the next two hours. At first shells only were used, but when we had got up to within 1,200 yards of Moultrie, grape shot could be used to advantage, the better to smother the enemy's fire.

It was felt that the situation of the *Lehigh* was extremely critical. About mid-forenoon Admiral Dahlgren came on board the *Nahant*, being rowed to her in his barge, and he at once took charge of the efforts being made to get a line to the *Lehigh* so that she could be assisted by towing, and a strenuous attempt was made to get her afloat again at the next high tide, which was near at hand. Dr. Langshaw, surgeon of the *Lehigh*, rowed by two men, came to the side of the *Nahant* twice with a line to take hold of our big hawser, but the line parted each time as soon as the "drag" of that heavy hawser came upon it. Then volunteers were called for, to row our little dinghy to the *Lehigh* with a stronger line. Horatio Young, seaman, Wm. Williams, and Frank S. Gile, landsmen, were first to come forward and ask to be allowed to make the attempt. They rowed the tiny boat through a rain of shot, shell, and grapeshot, handed the end of the line to men on the *Lehigh* and returned to the *Nahant* in safety. Admiral Dahlgren stepped forward and thanked them, congratulated them upon their success, and promoted them at once—Young to be petty officer, Williams and Gile to be able seamen.

Our heavy 13-inch hawser had been broken out from the storeroom, one end of it passed through the turret-chamber, up into the turret and then out the XI-inch gun-port to the deck, and our men lifted it across the deck upon its way as the line drew it off towards the *Lehigh*. Practically all of our men were needed to hand up and pass on that massive hawser. With much effort the end of it was safely drawn to the *Lehigh* and made fast, while we secured the other end around the armored base of our smokestack (having no bitts for such purpose), and then the pulling began.

The *Lehigh* had evidently been crowded onto the shoal by the inflowing tide, and had settled into the quicksand somewhat. The engines of both vessels were set going at full speed ahead, and after a little time it could be seen that we were gaining an inch, then another inch, then "a long pull, a strong pull, and a pull all together" did the trick, and the stranded monitor floated clear of the dangerous shoal about eleven o'clock to the great relief of everybody on the Union vessels. In a short time all the monitors withdrew from action and steamed down to the anchorage opposite Fort Wagner.

A few days later the following order was read at General Muster:

Flag Steamer *Philadelphia*,
Off Morris Island, November 17, 1863.

It is a gratifying duty to observe and make known the conduct of officers and men which obviously deserves such notice, particularly under fire.

The *Lehigh* grounded yesterday within good range of the enemy, and during the whole forenoon was under a very heavy fire of shot and shell from cannon and mortars. The *Nahant* in assisting her to float was also much exposed.

I can myself bear witness that nothing could have been better than the deportment of the commanders, officers, and men of both vessels under such trying circumstances.

Acting Ensign Richard Burk, who is severely wounded, is spoken of by his commanding officer in the official Report, who also mentions an indispensable service that demands special notice.

Three times a line to pass a hawser was conveyed from the *Nahant* to the *Lehigh*, twice by Dr. Langshaw, the surgeon of the *Lehigh*, and once by three seamen of the *Nahant*, Horatio Young, William Williams & Frank S. Gile. The latter I advanced in rate on the spot. The seamen of the *Lehigh*, George W. Leland, gunner's mate, Thos. Irving, Coxswain, who rowed Dr. Langshaw, will be also advanced a rate, and I shall also make honorable mention of them to the honorable Secretary of the Navy, which is all I can do for Dr. Langshaw. It is not in my power to reward him suitably.

This order will be read on every quarter-deck of the fleet at the next general muster after its reception.

John A. Dahlgren,
Rear Admiral, Comdg.[3]

3. General Order of Rear Admiral Dahlgren, 17 November 1863. ORN, I, 15:120.

17 | A Good Thanksgiving Dinner
The Story of the "Pickled Eels' Feet
The Fate of the *Weehawken*
My Time Expired

T HE NEXT DAY AFTER OUR STRENUOUS TIME WHEN THE *LEHIGH* WAS aground, the body of a man was seen floating past on the outgoing tide. One of our boats was sent after it and when the body was towed alongside it was found to be that of a negro. Most probably the body had floated down from Charleston. There was nothing that could be done, so the body was sent on shore for burial.

The heavy bombardment of Fort Sumter by the land batteries continued regularly, and usually two of the monitors were engaged in firing at the sea-face of the fort each day. As the *Nahant* had no rifled gun, she was only now and then ordered to this work, but she was sent up-channel on picket duty two nights out of three. An interesting experience it was on those nights to watch the great mortar shells which the Union batteries were now firing at Sumter, or which Moultrie and the Confederate batteries were firing at the Union batteries on Morris Island. And those shells could not only be seen, but we could hear the "sputter" of the burning fuses as the shells were climbing upward and then descending toward the target.

An amusing story was told of a negro on Morris Island who was seen crouching behind some simple shelter, and when he was laughed at for being afraid of those distant shells he said: "They's arfter me, Massa! They's arfter me!" When assured that it was quite impossible that the shells were "arfter" him he declared: "Yis they is, Massa, they keeps a sayin' 'Whar is yer, whar is yer?'"; and that phrase, spoken slowly and with the "is" soft, gives a very good idea of the sound of the burning shell-fuse as we used to hear it.

We would see the flash of the mortar, then, in a few seconds, would hear the "boom," and at about the same time the fuse-sparks would be seen. When the shell was at the apex of its flight and revolving slowly, the sound of the sputtering fuse would be softened by distance, but the sound steadily increased as the shell descended towards the earth. Also, the revolutions of the shell would be very slow when it was at the apex of its flight, and they would increase in rapidity as the speed of the shell increased in its descent.

Two days before Thanksgiving, the supply steamer *Massachusetts* arrived bringing, among the other supplies, a stock of turkeys. Our caterer consulted with steward Kruger, and then secured two fine turkeys for the wardroom mess. Kruger laid himself out to prepare an especially good dinner, and I had the satisfaction of being asked to assist him in making pies, cake, cookies, etc. Not that I could "help" much, but I could stir the messes the steward wanted stirred, could chop the mince meat, pare and chop the apples, etc., for Kruger had determined that he would have some "real" mince pies for this feast. He wasn't content to make pies of the "stuff" (as he called it) which the caterer had bought at Hilton Head as prepared mince-meat. One batch of so-called mince pies had been made of the prepared stuff, but they were not popular when served at mess; most of the pieces were left on the plates after one or two mouthfuls had been tried.

And so we chopped and mixed and stirred, and in due time half a dozen brown and savory-smelling mince pies were brought from the galley ovens and put away on the top shelf of the pantry. A barrel of apples and another of potatoes had been bought from the *Massachusetts*, cooked squash in tins we had in stock, and the array of "things good to eat" which were stored in the wardroom pantry for Thanksgiving would satisfy the ambition of even a New England housewife.

Nor was the crew unprovided for. Over 400 pounds of fresh beef had been bought and the best of it kept in our huge icebox for the Thanksgiving dinner of the men. Potatoes and onions were cooked to go with the boiled beef, and the berthdeck messes sat down to a dinner that was both appetizing and filling. Some of the messes had provided themselves with butter, purchased with money in their mess-funds, and there was no limit excepting shortage in those mess-funds to the good things the berthdeck messes could enjoy. Supply-steamers from the north visited the fleet twice a month, and there were "sutler's schooners" within reach almost always.

On Thanksgiving Day all the captains of naval vessels were invited to dine with the Admiral on board the flagship, which took away one member of the wardroom mess and brought the doctor into the chair at the head of the table. This change, however, in no way marred the enjoyment of the occasion. Indeed, the wardroom officers relaxed rather more than they might have felt free to do had the captain been at the table, and stories and jests went around in a manner which evidenced complete good fellowship.

The turkeys were nicely browned and steaming-hot, the vegetables were abundant and well cooked, the pies were praised to the steward's entire satisfaction, and when the fruit and nuts were set upon the table and the officers were left to themselves, nothing more was to be desired. For a half-hour or more the watch officer had left the deck in care of the senior quartermaster (the captain's permission to do this had been obtained), the assistant engineer on watch had come in from the engineroom to eat with the others, and the entire family was "present for duty," as the doctor humorously phrased it.

The wardroom cook in the galley fairly beamed with gratification that the dinner had gone off so well. True, conditions in the galley were more favorable with only two men working there than if there had been three cooks on duty: there was an advantage in the captain's now eating with the wardroom mess—there was no captain's cook in the galley, and steward Kruger had found it decidedly to his advantage to have the cabin pantry-space added to his storage room. He now "had room to do things," as he expressed it.

Regular supper was omitted on Thanksgiving evening, but cake and ginger snaps were set out on the table with canned peaches and plums, and a dish of preserved ginger-root, to any of which the officers helped themselves as they chose. When it came time for we boys to sit down to eat, I helped myself to a bit of the ginger-root and when I had tasted it had such an attack of laughter the other boys demanded to know what was the matter. Then I told them the story of Uncle Sam Wyley's "Pickled eels' feet."

Ten years before, when I was seven years old, father, mother, brother Charles, and I gad gone on a two-hundred-mile sleigh journey to Lincoln County, Maine, on a visit to father's old home and the Hunter relatives. At Grandpa Hunter's we found Captain and Aunt Caroline Wyley there on a visit, Aunt Caroline being father's youngest sister and married but a year or two. "Uncle Sam," as we called the captain, was very fond of "teasing" me, and in return for some trifling favor he had promised to give me some pickled eels' feet to eat. I stoutly maintained that eels had no feet, and that I knew they hadn't, because father had caught scores of eels in an eel-pot he used to set in a small river that bounded one side of his farm when we lived in Moultonboro! "But these are Chinese eels," said Uncle Sam. "The eels up in New Hampshire don't have feet, of course, but you'll see that Chinese eels *do* have feet, and I've some of those feet pickled. I'll convince you when I bring you some to eat!"

On a very stormy Sunday, when all the other grown-ups had gone to church and we two boys were left in care of Uncle Sam and Aunt Caroline, I began coaxing Uncle Sam to produce the "pickled eels' feet," and Aunt Caroline told him it was time that he should keep his promise. He took a saucer and spoon, disappeared down the cellar stairs, and in a few minutes returned with a saucer of conserve which was wholly new to me, but which I much enjoyed eating. When I tasted the preserved ginger-root on that Thanksgiving evening ten years later I instantly recognized it as Uncle Sam Wyley's "pickled eels' feet."

Sunday December 6th dawned bright and fair, and without any hint of a possible tragedy. A stiff breeze was blowing, heavy seas were breaking on the bar and considerable water washed over our deck as we lay at anchor. The hatch-coamings were on so that the hatches could be left off, and a few of the deadlight windsails were on so that the air below was comparatively fresh and good. After dinner was over, I sat at the wardroom table writing letters home, and in two of those letters made mention that my year's enlistment would expire two days later, but that I liked the service and intended to re-enlist for another year.

I finished, sealed and stamped my letters, then started to go on deck when I heard exclamations and shouts which hastened my steps, and got my head above the hatch-coaming in time to see the *Weehawken*, which was anchored two or three hundred yards distant, just sinking beneath the waves!

A few minutes earlier, a signal that assistance was wanted had been set on the *Weehawken*, then steam was seen to be coming from her engineroom hatchway. She was seen to heel over to starboard a little, then she settled beneath the surface bows first, righting herself as she rested upon the bottom, and two or three feet of the top of her smokestack showed above the surface of the water.

As I stood there by the berthdeck hatch, I could see men struggling in the water or clinging to the top of the smokestack, and half a score of boats (our 2d cutter among them) racing to the spot. The rescued men were taken aboard the flagship and cared for, and when our boat returned eager questions were asked, but there was little information that could be given. The sinking had been as great a surprise to the officers and men of the *Weehawken* as to those of us who saw it from a little distance, so great a surprise, indeed, that four of her officers and about twenty of the men were unable to get on deck to escape and went down in her; this was just about one-third of her crew.

And the horror of it grew upon me as I stood and gazed at the spot where the *Weehawken* had been, and the thought haunted me: "If the *Weehawken* today, why not the *Nahant* tomorrow, or next week, or next month!" Then there came over me the prophetic words of the old sailor on the *Ohio* nearly a year before: "Them new-fangled iron ships ain't fit for hogs to go to sea in, let alone honest sailors! You'll all go to the bottom in her, youngster, that's where you'll all go!"

After gazing and gazing at the top of the smokestack of the *Weehawken* for some time, and picturing the poor fellows lying down there in their iron coffin, I went down to the wardroom and tore up the two letters in which I had told the home-folks that I intended to re-enlist.

We on board the *Nahant* well *knew* what had caused the disaster to the *Weehawken*. We knew it was her being too heavily loaded forward, just as had been the case with the *Nahant* when we started out from Port Royal harbor nearly four weeks before. The *Nahant* had turned back to Port Royal and changed the trim of the ship by hoisting out a lot of heavy shot and moving them aft, so that the water coming into the windlass-room (and there was *some* water coming through the hawse-hole whenever we were in a sea-way) would flow aft to where the pumps could get hold of it. The officers of the *Weehawken* had not been sufficiently alert, the water coming in forward had been allowed to accumulate until it was above the windlass-room floor, and the ship was then so down by the head, nothing could be done to save her.

A court of inquiry which was held found that the causes of the sinking of the *Weehawken* were:

The additional weight of ammunition that had been lately put on board of her, leaving her trim so little by the stern as not

to allow sufficient inclination for water to get to the pumps
freely.

The neglect to close the hawse hole, and the delay in closing
the hatch over the windlass room, which permitted the rapid
accumulation at the forward extremity of the vessel of sufficient
water to bring her nearly on an even keel. [1]

And Captain Ammen's *The Atlantic Coast* says:

Five minutes before the vessel went down the signal was
made "Assistance required." At this moment no assistance could
be rendered, save to rescue the crew from drowning. The vessel
heeled over to the right, or, as seamen would say, "to starboard;"
the bow settled, the water within rushed forward; for a minute,
more or less, she lay on her side, gradually settling, the water
pouring in through the turret port, which was open, and
through the main hatch, over the "hopper;" a dense steam arose
out of the engine-room, the vessel assumed an upright position
as she went down, and the top of the smokestack alone remained
visible when the keel rested on the bottom. Four officers and
twenty men were drowned, being below at the time, and unable
to reach the deck through the inrush of the water, or, if on deck,
unable to keep themselves afloat for the few minutes that
intervened until boats were at hand for their rescue. [2]

All of the next day the disaster to the *Weehawken* was practically
the sole topic of conversation, and the many rumors flying about were
discussed by the groups which formed now and then as opportunity
afforded. Just about sunset a large, bark-rigged steamship came up to
and anchored near the *Wabash*, and my inquiry as to what steamer she
was brought the information that she was the *Circassian*, supply
steamer to the West-Gulf Blockading Squadron, on her way north and
probably had stopped to take on the mail. Instinctively the thought
came to me: "I'm going home on that steamer." [3]

The next morning, Tuesday, December 8th, I turned my gaze
seaward as soon as I stepped on deck with the watch-officer's cup of

1. Finding of the Court of Enquiry. ORN, I, 15:167. Ironically, Commander Jesse
Duncan had replaced Commander Edmund R. Colhoun as commanding officer of the
Weehawken only the day before.

2. Ammen, 144–45.

3. The *Circassian* was an iron hulled screw steamer captured by Union naval forces
while attempting to run the blockade in May 1862. It was purchased by the government
and taken into Federal service in November. In 1863, its commander was Acting
Volunteer Lieutenant E. W. Eaton.

coffee, and there lay the bark-rigged steamship, just as my hopes had promised. I gleefully told the quartermaster that my time expired that morning and I expected to go north on the *Circassian* to be discharged. This was, of course, a wild guess, because there were two men on board whose time had expired more than two months before and others whose time had expired since so there were as many as ten or a dozen on board who were entitled to be discharged. Because of the shortage of men in the fleet, however, these men had not been sent north.

At eight bells (eight o'clock) I went to the officer of the deck, saluted, and reported that my term of enlistment expired that day. Pilot Sofield was officer of the deck, and I watched him gravely reach up his hand for the log-slate and then write upon it the important item that: "Alvah Hunter, Boy, reported the expiration of his term of enlistment." Two others, Chas. Snellen and Wm. H. Kruger (the wardroom steward), also reported their terms as expired that day.

About mid-forenoon the boatswain's whistle sounded, and the order was passed for those whose time had expired to muster on deck, and eleven of us assembled there. We were told that we were to be transferred to the *Circassian* about noon, and to be ready with our bags and hammocks to go to her, also that the paymaster would advance ten dollars to each man on his pay account. Then one of the eleven said he didn't care to go home before spring anyway, and couldn't we volunteer to stay with the ship for six months?

The desire to stay with the ship through the winter seemed contagious, and we all signed a paper stating that we didn't want to go north before spring, that we much desired to stay and help capture Fort Sumter, and that we would re-ship for a term of six months and stay on the *Nahant*. The paper was taken to the Captain, who was told of the feeling among the men, and Captain Cornwall went to the flagship to report the matter to the Admiral. Half an hour later he returned with a message of thanks to the men, and the statement that "The enlistment law didn't allow of shipments being made for any period of less than one year, and that the Admiral wasn't able to accept 'voluntary service' because there was no 'emergency need' of such service. He hoped, however, that such valiant and patriotic men as we had shown ourselves to be would re-enlist for the year."

The enthusiasm to stay had already begun to cool and this message still further cooled it. None wanted to stay in those waters through another summer, and in the afternoon all eleven of us shouldered our bags and hammocks and went aboard the tug, bidding our shipmates and the good ship *Nahant* an affectionate good-bye as the tug cast off and steamed away.

The tug went from ship to ship taking aboard men whose time had expired, and it was sunset when we finally steamed out over the bar and I climbed the long Jacob's Ladder which brought me to the deck of the *Circassian*. There was a quite heavy sea running and the bobbing of the tugboat had upset me, so, without waiting to get supper, I hurried down the companionway to the 'tween-decks, selected a vacant bunk quite well forward, spread my hammock and mattress and "turned in all-standing."

18 ‖ Homeward Bound

A Blockade Runner Captured and a Visit to Her

The Voyage to Boston

Paid Off and Discharged.

To say that I was "dead tired" when I turned in on board the *Circassian* about five o'clock in the evening of Tuesday, December 8th, 1863, does scant justice to my condition. The excitement and mental strain caused by the sinking of the *Weehawken* on Sunday afternoon had pretty much denied me sleep for two nights, and the sudden attack of seasickness as the tugboat crossed the bar when conveying us out to the *Circassian* had brought me to a state of complete exhaustion. It is not at all strange that I more than "slept the clock around."

About six o'clock the next morning I was awakened by the sound of a gun, which seemed to be just over my head, and in a few seconds I was up the companionway to the main deck to see what was doing. I had turned in "all standing" the evening before, hence didn't have to stop to dress before going on deck. Day-break was just lightening the eastern sky and a half-mile distant was a three-masted steamer slowing down in response to a shot from our bow gun that summoned her to heave-to. Her masts had the familiar "rakish slant" which was so much affected by the English builders of blockade-running steamers, and the fact that she stood so high out of the water told us that she had been intending to run into some Confederate port for a cargo; she wasn't outward-bound with a full cargo. The further fact that she was headed off-shore when discovered was explained by her having failed to get near enough to shore to make a dash for a harbor the night before, and she was standing off to the eastward under slow speed to await the coming of another night. [1]

The *Circassian* had headed outward the night before so as to the sooner get the benefit of the northward current of the Gulf Stream. Her lookout had discovered this steamer standing off-shore in the early morning light and we had crept up on her out of the darkness without her officers imagining there was a United States war ship within fifty miles. She could easily steam faster than the *Circassian's* nine or ten knots, and but for the protecting darkness to the westward we never would have got near enough to that steamer to make her heave-to.

The sight of the captured blockade-runner near at hand was intensely interesting. I could have hugged myself with delight at having so unexpectedly come upon a real adventure: to be in at the capture of a steamer on the very first day of our homeward voyage was rare good luck. As I stood at the rail, watching, we were gradually drawing nearer our prize, our engine having been stopped when we were perhaps a quarter-mile away. By the time we were within an eighth of a mile and nearly stopped, one of the boats had been swung out ready to be lowered, and three officers and half a dozen armed men were in the waist ready to board the prize. One of the assistant engineers went in the boat, and there was evidently need of haste, for a cloud of steam which was flowing from the steamer's smokestack looked suspicious.

As the boat drew near the steamer the officer in command stood up and hailed her, a second and then a third hail was necessary before any attention was given him, then a man's head appeared above the rail for a moment, and in response to the officer's demand a line was thrown over the side. One of the men climbed aboard with the aid of the line and in a few minutes he lowered a ladder over the side, the officers climbed aboard, followed by the men, and then for fifteen or twenty minutes we watched for developments. These came in the shape of the junior officer coming down the ladder to the boat, which was hastily rowed back to the *Circassian* and the officer made report to the executive officer and captain.

Then a dozen men equipped with buckets went into the boat, which with the chief engineer and another assistant engineer, returned to the prize. After another wait the boatswain's whistle sounded and

1. The prize vessel was the British steamer *Minna* carrying iron, hardware, gunpowder, and some marine engine parts possibly intended for a Confederate ironclad to be built in Charleston.

call was made for all hands to muster on deck. When the men were assembled a list of names was called and the men named were ordered to go aboard the steamer as a prize crew. A little later a boatload of firemen and coalheavers was sent aboard the prize, then the boat returned and a working party of eight or ten men was sent on board to help in getting her into working condition.

When the first of this lot of men went over the side and down to the boat the thought came to me like a flash: "What fun it would be to go aboard that prize steamer and explore her!" Down the companionway I hurried and exchanged my cap, which had a band with "*Nahant*" in gold letters on it, for an every day cap which had no name-band, then walked along the deck to the ladder, down to the boat and took a seat in the bow just as though I belonged there. No one paid any attention to me, they all evidently took it for granted that I was one of the men ordered to the prize. My heart was in my mouth for a few minutes, with fear someone would notice that mine was a strange face, but probably the men of the *Circassian*'s crew were not well acquainted with each other; quite possibly many of them were (like myself) going north to be discharged and were helping at the work of the ship.

Few words were spoken as the boat was rowed over the heaving waves to the side of the prize and I took care to be the second man up the ladder, once over the rail I disappeared forward in quick time and dodged down in the companionway to the 'tweendecks. I certainly felt that I was a culprit of some sort, but determined to see as much as possible and fully deserve any punishment that might come to me, so began to explore the 'tweendecks and then went down into the forward hold.

This cavernous hold was innocent of cargo, but I had not groped about in the dim light many minutes before I discovered small packages of different kinds concealed in angles of the braces and other snug places, and one package which had broken open I saw contained several dozen pocket knives of English make. As I had accidentally broken my pocket knife a little while before, and as these odd bundles of goods were evidently "flyers" in blockade-run-goods being made by individual men of the steamer's crew, I selected a good knife and pocketed it. Those knives were certainly not listed on the steamer's manifest, hence were a legitimate prize for anybody who found them.

Hidden under some sacking I found a bag of what appeared to be oranges, but were of a much lighter yellow than any oranges I had ever seen. Quartering the skin of one I finally succeeded in removing it after much effort, broke the "orange" in halves, separated one of the sections and clapped it into my mouth,—to discover that I was attempting the bitterest piece of orange that I had ever tasted! The tears came into my eyes and my mouth watered freely, and get rid of that terribly bitter taste I could not for quite a while. Years later I learned that it was a "Shaddock" that I had attempted to eat as though it was an orange, and it was the Shaddock in its wild state; it was far different from the cultivated and greatly improved fruit which is now well known as Grape Fruit.

After some little more exploring of the hold, I returned to the 'tweendecks and investigated there. In the messroom of the crew I saw ten or a dozen more or less tipsy men, and on the opposite side of the deck I saw some men from the *Circassian* who were at work passing along and dumping through an open port buckets of water which were being passed up from the fireroom.

I heard a day or two later that when the officers of the prize saw that their vessel was to be captured the men in the fireroom were ordered to draw the fires from the furnaces and drown them with water from a hose, the steam in the boilers was released and went up the funnel, and the sea-cocks were opened to let water into the after hold in the hope that the vessel would become waterlogged before working parties from the *Circassian* could get busy and save her from sinking.

The prompt action of the assistant engineer first aboard the prize had frustrated the plan. Sensing what had been done he put his revolver to the head of the least drunk of the engineers of the steamer and ordered him to close the sea-cocks instanter. This being done the rising water, already over the fireroom floor, was checked, but there wasn't steam in the boilers to work the pumps, so bailing with buckets was resorted to to get the water down so fires could be got going and steam to work the pumps could be made; then the water was soon got out of the hold.

Continuing my way aft, I came to an open door leading into the cabin and, as there seemed to be no one there, I entered. On the mess table were several bottles of wine and spirits, and on top of a locker was a case of wine which had apparently been smashed open when the officers decided to get as much booze as possible inside them before the Yankee boat came alongside. Possibly it also explained the failure of the steamer's running the blockade the night before. The half-to-two-thirds-drunk condition of officers and men doubtless accounted for the inhospitable reception given the boarding officer when the boat came alongside.

Another thing which I discovered on the cabin table was a tin of biscuits, and as it was now mid-forenoon, and I had had no breakfast (nor supper the night before) I gladly fisted as many of them as I could cram into my pockets, took a generous handful of them and withdrew, not, however, until one of the steamer's officers who was lying in a berth in one of the staterooms had spied me and called out: "Help 'self, young feller, Help 'self."

After I had strolled about a while longer and eaten the biscuits, I went on deck and came suddenly upon one of the officers from the *Circassian,* who demanded: "Why aren't you at work? What party do you belong to?" I told him I didn't belong to any working party, that I was simply "a boy" from the South Atlantic Squadron going north to be discharged, and had come aboard the prize just to have a look at her. Probably my rather small size, added to my perfect frankness, saved me. The expression on that youthful officer's face changed from indignation to surprise, then to amusement, and there was a merry look in his eyes as he said: "Well, There's a boat down there, (pointing aft towards the ladder), that's going back to the *Circassian* in a few minutes, and *you* go back in it!" I saluted and said: "Aye, aye, Sir!" and walked aft to the ladder, but heard his sotto-voce remark: "And you better keep your mouth shut!" Needless to add I did keep my mouth shut, and no one on board the *Circassian* learned of my adventure from me.

The two steamships lay within a cable's length of each other all day, the boat going back and forth now and then with supplies, tools, men, etc. Late in the afternoon it was rumored that the engine of the prize had been "queered"; a hawser was got out and the end passed to her, the *Circassian* took her in tow and again headed north. The current of the Gulf Stream had been steadily floating us north all day, but it was comforting to be again steaming ahead and feel that we were really "going home". Then came a new trouble in the form of an order that we men who were homeward bound must turn-to and help work the ship because it was short handed.

The growling amongst the old salts was most amusing. We were not carried on the ship's muster roll, hence were not in line for a share of the prize money which would accrue from the capture of the blockade runner, and yet we were ordered to fill the places of the men who had been sent on board the prize to work her into port; it looked to be quite unfair. When we mustered on deck I found myself assigned to the port watch, which would stand the first watch, going on duty at eight bells.

I felt decidedly indignant at being ordered to deck duty, and studied the problem of how I could avoid it without seeming to be mutinous. Not having decided upon a course of action, I fell in line with the port watch and answered when my name was called. A dozen of us were ordered to the ashes-hoist to get up and dump overboard the ashes in the fireroom. I followed along to the side and tailed into the tackle, but seemed to be in the way rather than a help, so stepped back a little to watch the others. Realizing that I was somewhat like a fifth wheel to that coach I slipped away down the companionway, went to my bunk and turned in.

I had taken some cold, my throat was sore and I was amply hoarse, so I answered the sick-call next morning by going to the dispensary. The doctor felt my pulse, looked at my tongue and into my throat, gave me a few powders to take, and told me to come to the dispensary three times during the day to gargle my throat with a mixture the dispensary steward would give me, and to keep quiet and get rested. I tossed the powders overboard as soon as I was out of sight of the dispensary, but reported a couple of times for the gargle, and fully obeyed the instruction to keep quiet and rest.

Late in the afternoon Kruger came forward to my bunk to ask after my welfare, having heard the pother when I failed to answer to my name at roll call, and while we were talking the master-at-arms came along looking for "Hunter". In a hoarse voice I told him I was sick and in the doctor's hands, and that the doctor had ordered me to keep quiet, but the master-at-arms began to accuse me of "sojering", told me to get up and go on duty or he'd. . . . Then Kruger came to my defence and told him I was only a boy anyway and couldn't rightly be made to do deck duty. This was a new idea to me, a new line of defence, and I kept quiet to see what would be the outcome. The petty officer demanded to know if I wasn't really "a landsman", and said that most of the boys were really rated as landsmen (which was quite true), but Kruger quietly assured him that my rating was that of 1st-class boy, and that I had been one of his wardroom boys on the *Nahant*, and in disgust the master-at-arms crossed my name off the list of port-watch men and departed.

After thus getting free of deck duty, the ships grub, which wasn't at all to my liking and was decidedly below the food served to the men on board the *Nahant*, became a subject of worry to me, and I wondered if there wasn't some way by which I could get better food. After thinking it over, I went to the galley and interviewed the wardroom cook. I told him I had been a wardroom boy on the *Nahant* and asked him if he couldn't put aside for me some food from that he was daily handling. Manifestly he was no stranger to the proposition and he soon acknowledged that he *might* be able to help me. Then he asked if I had any money. I had a dollar in fractional currency and a brand new ten dollar bill, the latter Mr. Putnam had advanced me on my pay-account, so I quickly demonstrated to the cook that I was both able and willing to pay for good food—for the remainder of the voyage I had my private supply.

For the first day and a half of our voyage the weather was considerably rough, but by the afternoon of December 11th the wind calmed down so that there was less discomfort, and that evening the prize steamer was got into condition to steam ahead at moderate speed, but we still kept her in tow. Better progress was now made and early the next morning we steamed in past Cape Henry, and about eight o'clock we dropped anchor near Fortress Monroe. The *Circassian* had turned in to Hampton Roads to report to the Navy Department in Washington and await orders.

In the afternoon a tugboat came alongside with some fifty plantation negroes ("Contrabands"[2]), on board, and they were put aboard, the *Circassion* for transportation to Boston. They had practically no baggage—half a dozen had a few things tied up in bandanna handkerchiefs—and their clothing was the simple jumpers and trousers of cotton cloth which they had worn when they came into the Union lines. What these southern-bred negroes would do in the cold of a Boston winter was an interesting question. About four o'clock in the afternoon the anchor was hoisted and we steamed away for Boston, the prize steamer being left there in Hampton Roads for the disposal of the prize court.

For the three following days we had head winds and a rough sea, and Monday, the 14th, we were hove to several hours on account of the

---

2. Major General Benjamin Butler was the first to use the term "contraband" to describe the runaway slaves that came into the Union lines. His argument was that since the enemy often used slaves to dig fortifications, the Union forces were justified in refusing to return them to their owners since they were "contraband of war."

dense fog. By dead reckoning we were then about seventy miles south-west of Gay Head, Martha's Vineyard. The next day the weather was thick and rainy, but less foggy; we steamed slowly through Vineyard Sound and just before dark came to anchor in Holmes' Hole, now called Vineyard Haven. The morning of the 16th opened fair, with a north-west wind. We got underway at daybreak, passed Cape Cod about four o'clock in the afternoon and headed across Massachusetts Bay for Boston Light.

It was bitterly cold as we pushed right into the teeth of a strong head wind, and soon after supper I turned in for the sake of the warmth of my blankets, to be awakened three hours later by the rattle of the anchor chain racing through the hawse pipe just as four bells struck. "Ten o'clock!" I exclaimed. "That means Boston!" In an instant I was out of my bunk and hurried up the companionway to the deck, to be greeted by the sight of glorious old Bunker Hill Monument, standing out sharp and clear in the bright moonlight. I let out a happy laugh—this was "home!"

It snowed, rained, and hailed in true Boston style all day on the 17th, rained all that night, and it was still raining when a tugboat came alongside the *Circassian* about noon of the 18th and conveyed us to the receiving ship *Ohio*. Men in the United States Navy were regularly "transferred" from one ship to another, and time was necessary for making out the pay accounts of the hundred men or so that had been brought north on the *Circassian*, and it was mid-afternoon of Saturday, December 19th, that we were at last mustered on deck and formed in line in the order in which our names were called. We were then marched down to the paymaster's office, where we were told to "touch the pen" as a clerk wrote each name on the pay roll, then another clerk counted out the amount of pay due each one and handed it to him, together with a regular discharge from the United States Navy. My year and ten day's service, at $8. per month, netted me $98.67, of which sum I had drawn ten dollars when leaving the *Nahant*, and I tucked $88.67 away in my pocket along with my discharge.

Getting my bag and hammock I presented myself at the gangway to go onshore, which I was permitted to do as soon as a corporal of marines had inspected my discharge and looked me over sharply to see if my appearance tallied with the description given of me in that document. Again on the landing stage my discharge was inspected, and at the gate of the Navy Yard another corporal of marines looked me over carefully before he handed my discharge back and signified that I was free to walk out.

Hoisting my hammock to my shoulder and getting my clothes bag under the other arm, I trudged up Bunker Hill, across the Monument Grounds and down Bartlett Street to Aunt Folsom's door, walked in and was "HOME".

THE END.

‖ Index